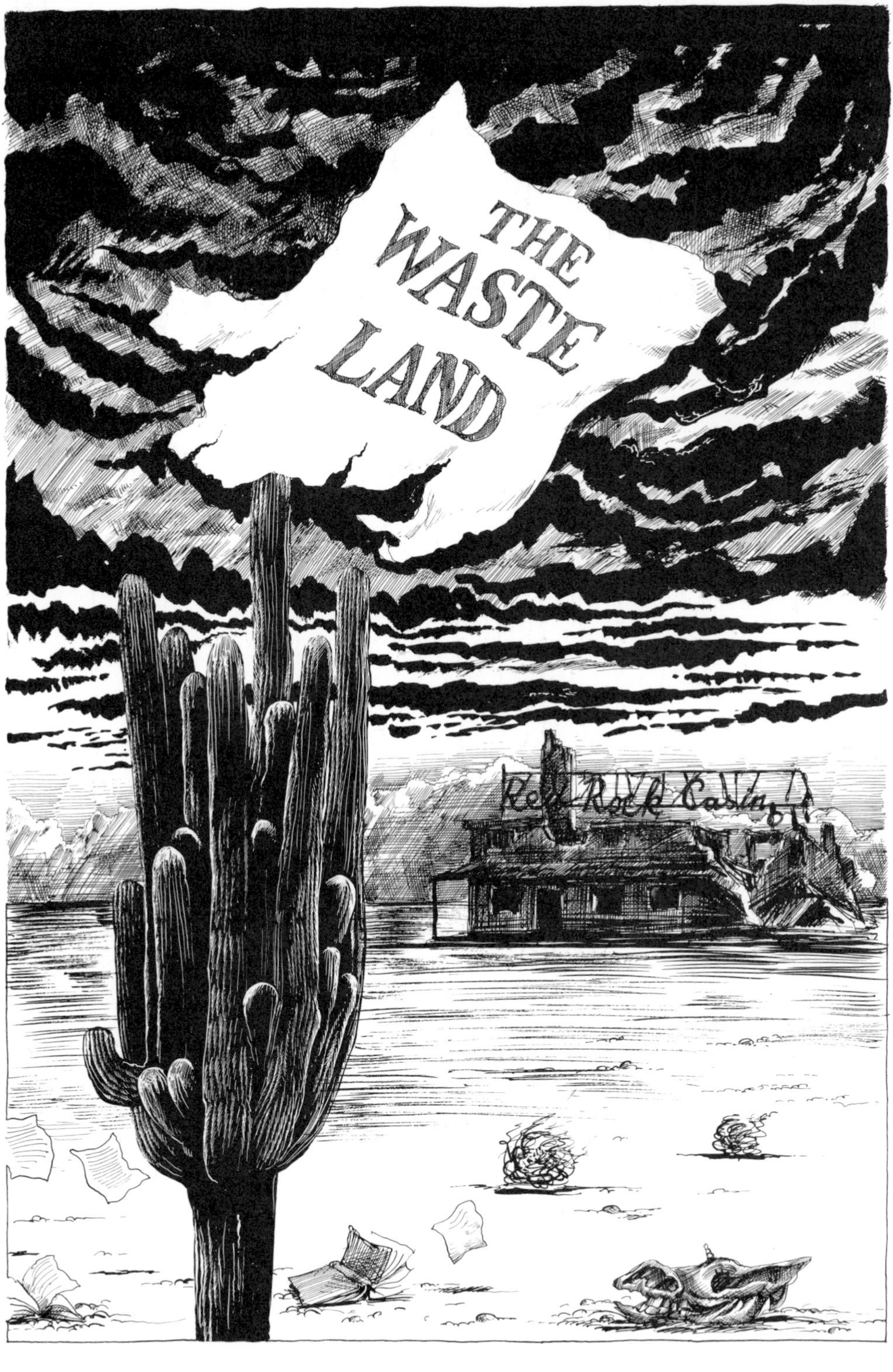
THE
WASTE
LAND
Red Rock Casino!

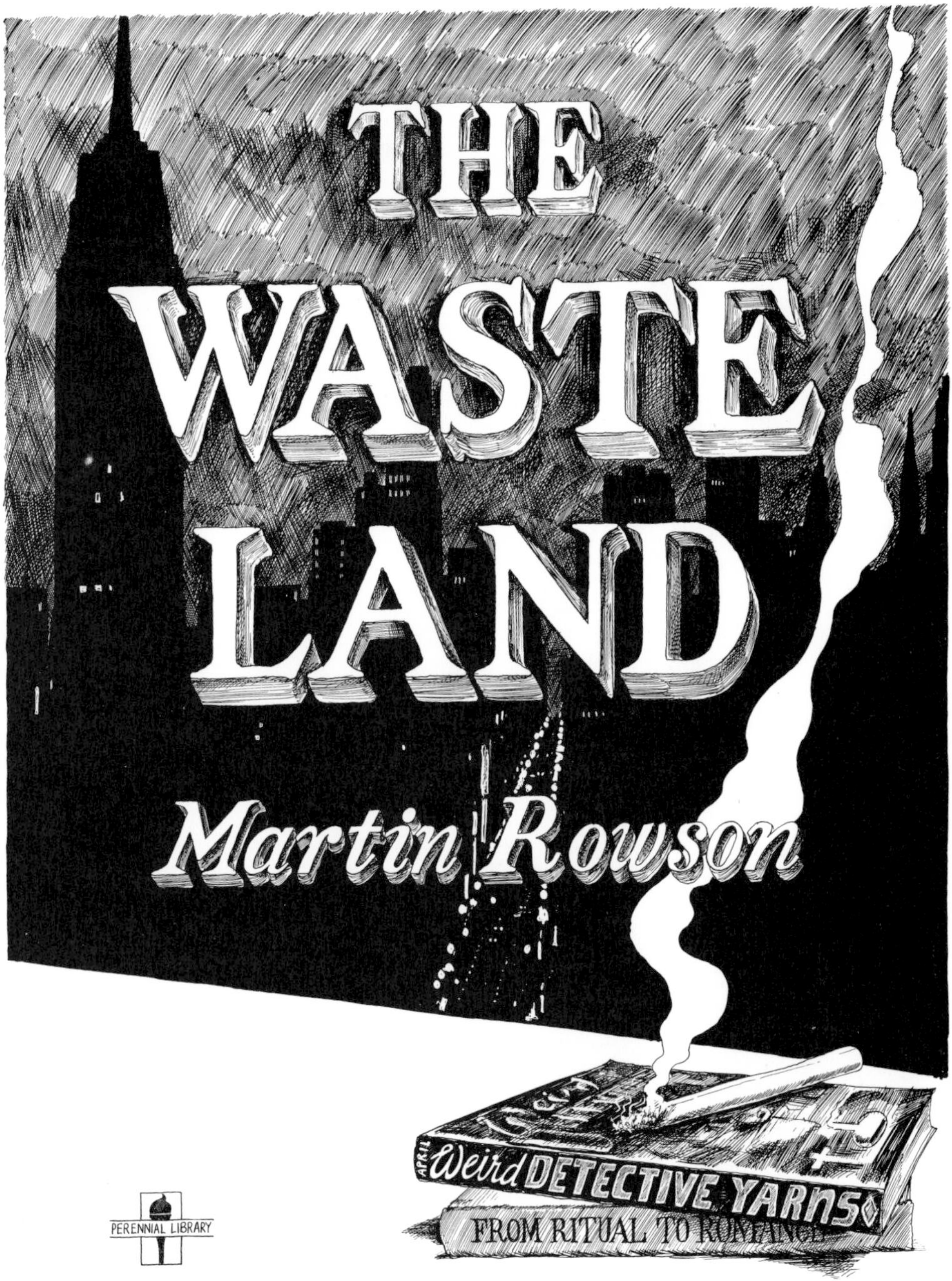
THE
WASTE
LAND
Martin Rowson
APRIL
Weird DETECTIVE YARNS
FROM RITUAL TO ROMANCE

PERENNIAL LIBRARY

An Edward Burlingame Book

HARPER & ROW, PUBLISHERS, NEW YORK,
GRAND RAPIDS, PHILADELPHIA, ST. LOUIS, SAN FRANCISCO
LONDON, SINGAPORE, SYDNEY, TOKYO, TORONTO

First PERENNIAL LIBRARY edition published 1990.

LIBRARY OF CONGRESS CATALOG CARD NUMBER 89-45711

ISBN 0-06-096476-6

90 91 92 93 94 MPC 10 9 8 7 6 5 4 3 2

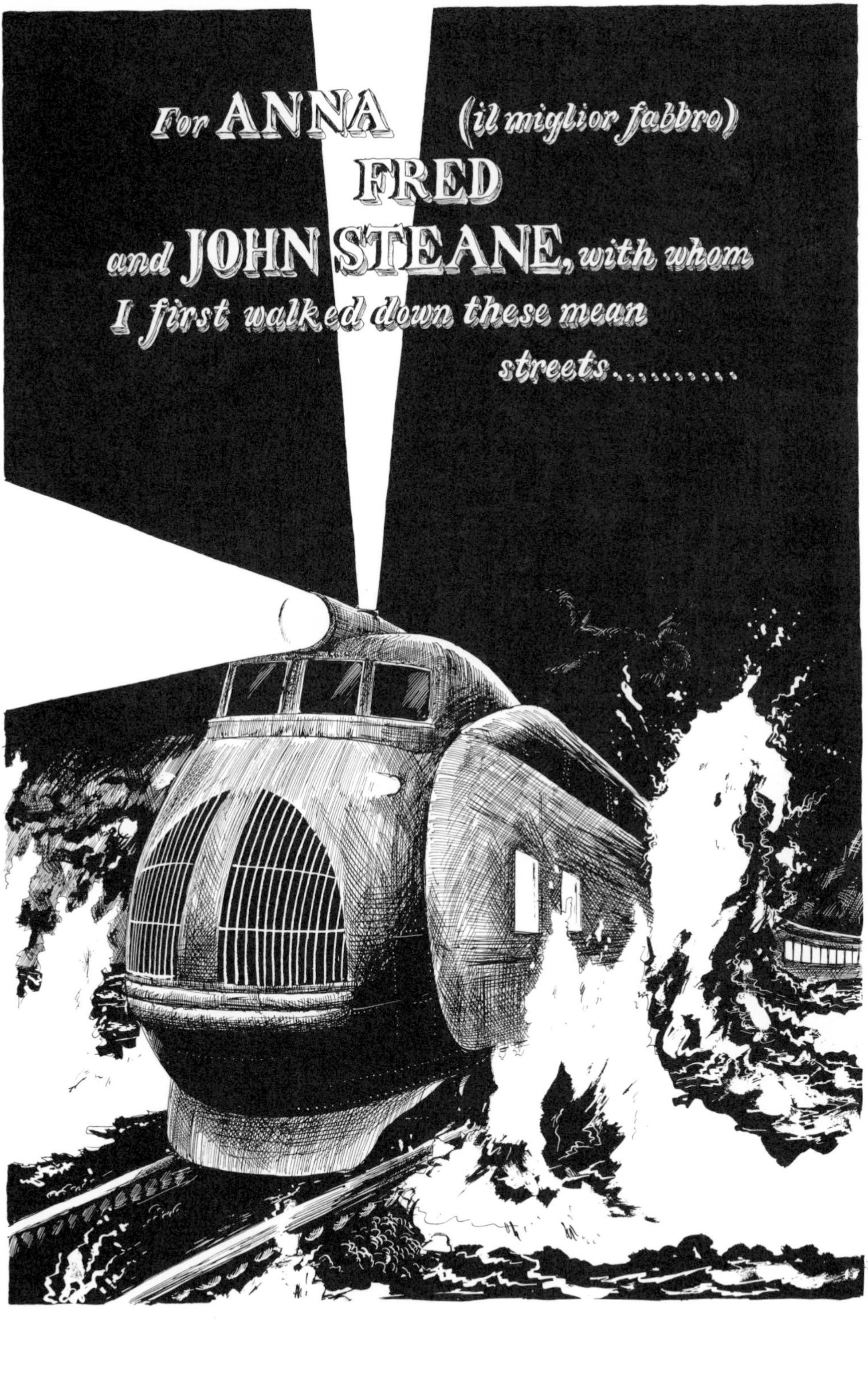
For ANNA (il miglior fabbro)
FRED
and JOHN STEANE, with whom
I first walked down these mean
streets..........

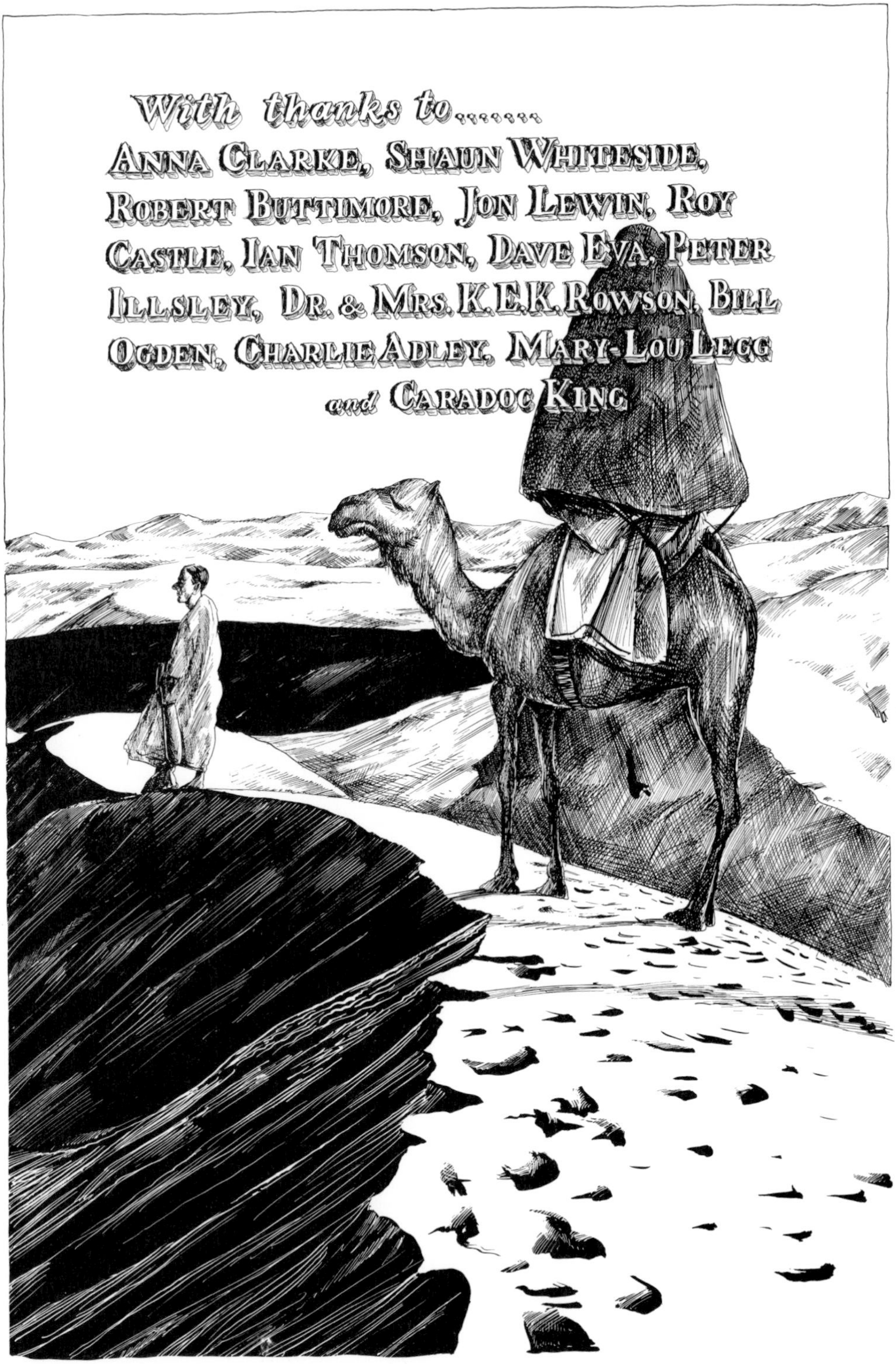
With thanks to........
Anna Clarke, Shaun Whiteside, Robert Buttimore, Jon Lewin, Roy Castle, Ian Thomson, Dave Eva, Peter Illsley, Dr. & Mrs. K.E.K. Rowson, Bill Ogden, Charlie Adley, Mary-Lou Legg and Caradoc King

Then there is the pale, pale blonde with anæmia of some non-fatal but incurable type. She is very languid and very shadowy and she speaks softly out of nowhere and you can't lay a finger on her because in the first place you don't want to and in the second place she is reading THE WASTE LAND *or Dante in the original, or Kafka or Kierkegaard or studying Provençal......*

Raymond Chandler, THE LONG GOODBYE

"May I ask Mr Marlowe a question?"

"Certainly, Amos."

He put down the overnight case inside the door and she went in past me and left us.

"'I grow old... I grow old... I shall wear the bottoms of my trousers rolled.' What does that mean, Mr Marlowe?"

"Not a bloody thing. It just sounds good."

He smiled. "That is from the Love Song of J. Alfred Prufrock. Here's another one. 'In the room the women come and go Talking of Michelangelo.' Does that suggest anything to you, sir?"

"Yeah – it suggests to me that the guy didn't know very much about women."

"My sentiments exactly, sir. Nonetheless I admire T. S. Eliot very much."

"Did you say 'nonetheless'?"

Raymond Chandler, THE LONG GOODBYE

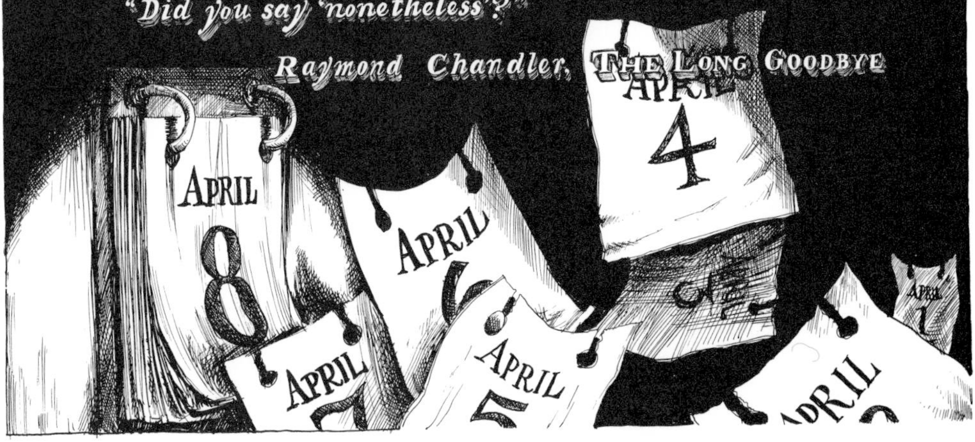
APRIL
8
APRIL
4
APRIL
APRIL
APRIL

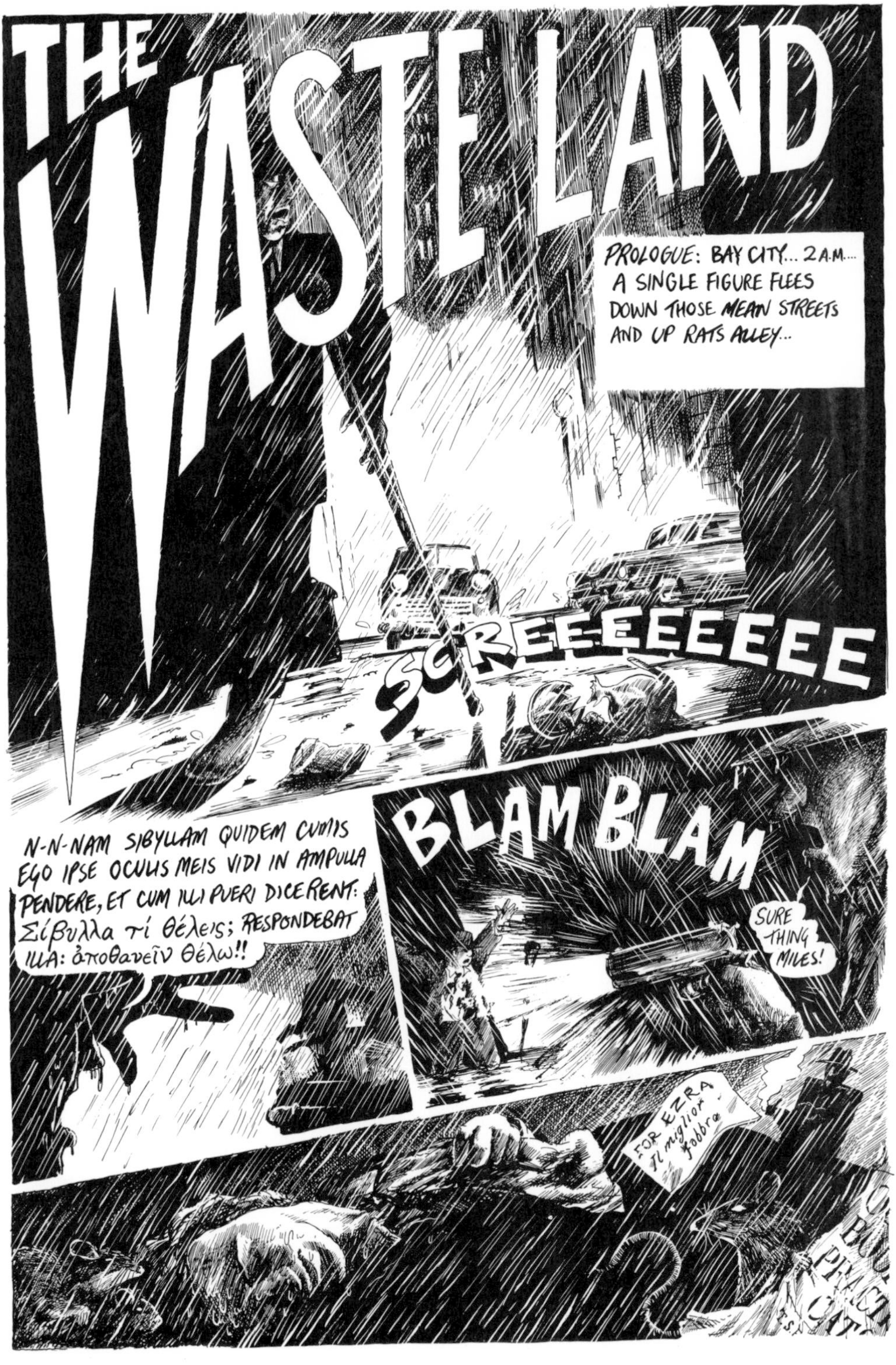
THE WASTE LAND
PROLOGUE: BAY CITY... 2 A.M.... A SINGLE FIGURE FLEES DOWN THOSE MEAN STREETS AND UP RATS ALLEY...
SCREEEEEEEEE
BLAM BLAM
N-N-NAM SIBYLLAM QUIDEM CUMIS EGO IPSE OCULIS MEIS VIDI IN AMPULLA PENDERE, ET CUM ILLI PUERI DICERENT: Σίβυλλα τί θέλεις; RESPONDEBAT ILLA: ἀποθανεῖν θέλω!!
SURE THING MILES!
FOR EZRA Il miglior fabbro

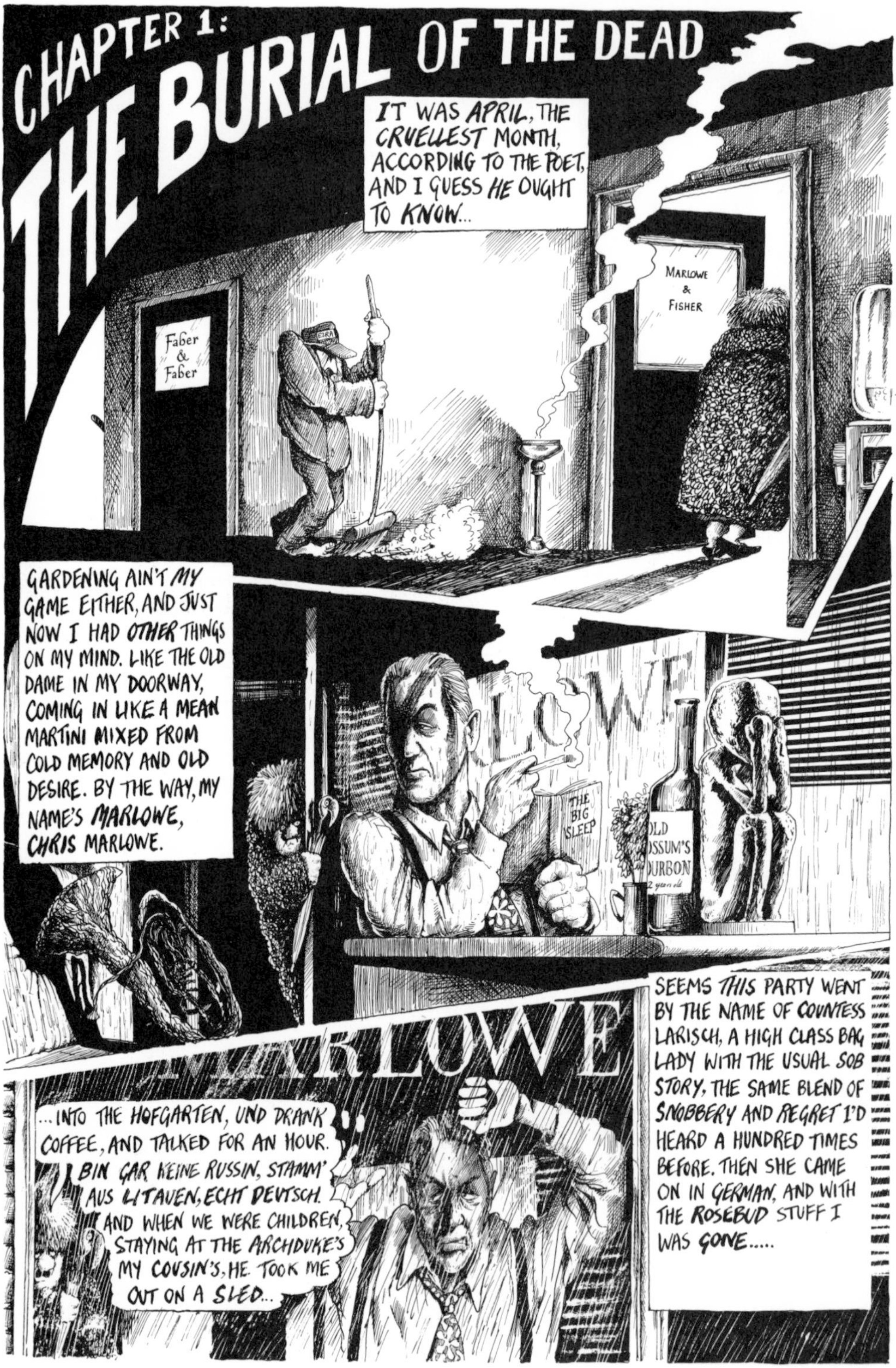
CHAPTER 1: THE BURIAL OF THE DEAD
IT WAS APRIL, THE CRUELLEST MONTH, ACCORDING TO THE POET, AND I GUESS HE OUGHT TO KNOW...
Faber & Faber
MARLOWE & FISHER
GARDENING AIN'T MY GAME EITHER, AND JUST NOW I HAD OTHER THINGS ON MY MIND. LIKE THE OLD DAME IN MY DOORWAY, COMING IN LIKE A MEAN MARTINI MIXED FROM COLD MEMORY AND OLD DESIRE. BY THE WAY, MY NAME'S MARLOWE, CHRIS MARLOWE.
THE BIG SLEEP
SEEMS THIS PARTY WENT BY THE NAME OF COUNTESS LARISCH, A HIGH CLASS BAG LADY WITH THE USUAL SOB STORY, THE SAME BLEND OF SNOBBERY AND REGRET I'D HEARD A HUNDRED TIMES BEFORE. THEN SHE CAME ON IN GERMAN, AND WITH THE ROSEBUD STUFF I WAS GONE.....
...INTO THE HOFGARTEN, UND DRANK COFFEE, AND TALKED FOR AN HOUR. BIN GAR KEINE RUSSIN, STAMM' AUS LITAUEN, ECHT DEUTSCH. AND WHEN WE WERE CHILDREN, STAYING AT THE ARCHDUKE'S MY COUSIN'S, HE TOOK ME OUT ON A SLED...
MARLOWE

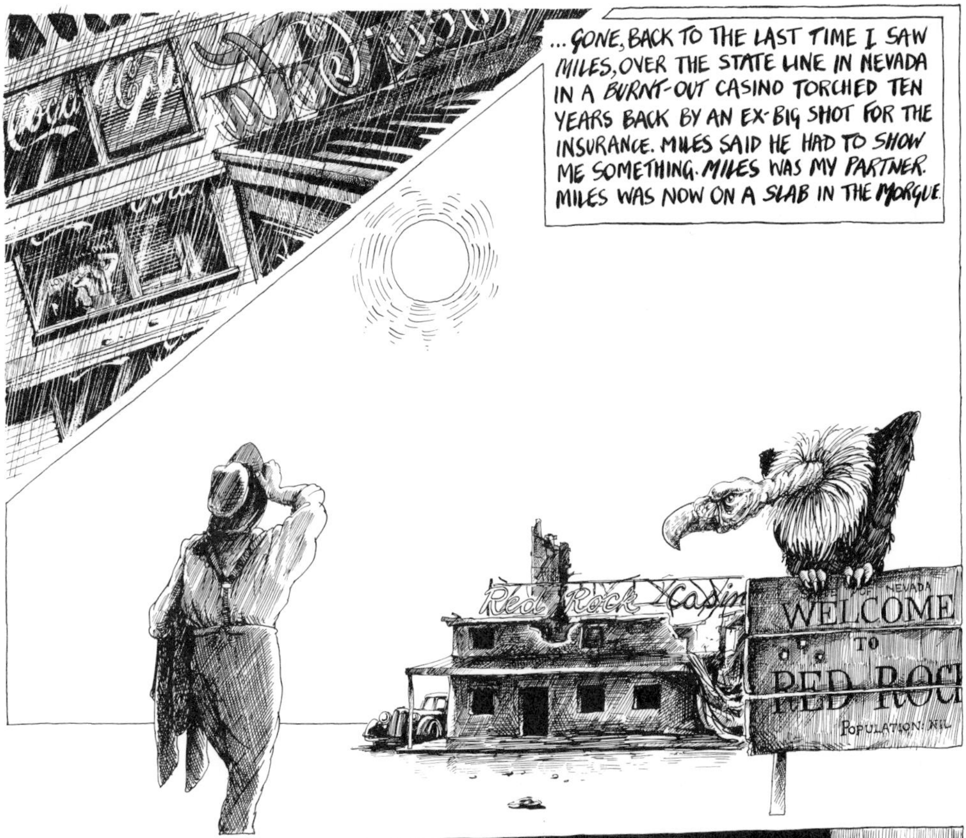
...GONE, BACK TO THE LAST TIME I SAW MILES, OVER THE STATE LINE IN NEVADA IN A BURNT-OUT CASINO TORCHED TEN YEARS BACK BY AN EX-BIG SHOT FOR THE INSURANCE. MILES SAID HE HAD TO SHOW ME SOMETHING. MILES WAS MY PARTNER. MILES WAS NOW ON A SLAB IN THE MORGUE.
Red Rock Casino
NEVADA
WELCOME
TO
POPULATION: NIL

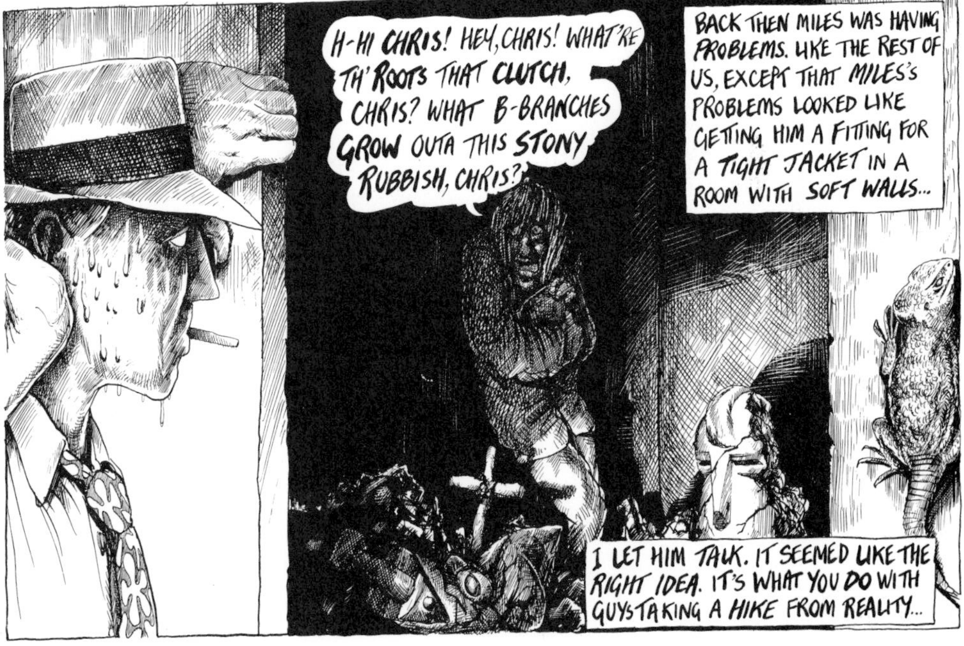
H-HI CHRIS! HEY, CHRIS! WHAT'RE TH' ROOTS THAT CLUTCH, CHRIS? WHAT B-BRANCHES GROW OUTA THIS STONY RUBBISH, CHRIS?
BACK THEN MILES WAS HAVING PROBLEMS. LIKE THE REST OF US, EXCEPT THAT MILES'S PROBLEMS LOOKED LIKE GETTING HIM A FITTING FOR A TIGHT JACKET IN A ROOM WITH SOFT WALLS...
I LET HIM TALK. IT SEEMED LIKE THE RIGHT IDEA. IT'S WHAT YOU DO WITH GUYS TAKING A HIKE FROM REALITY...

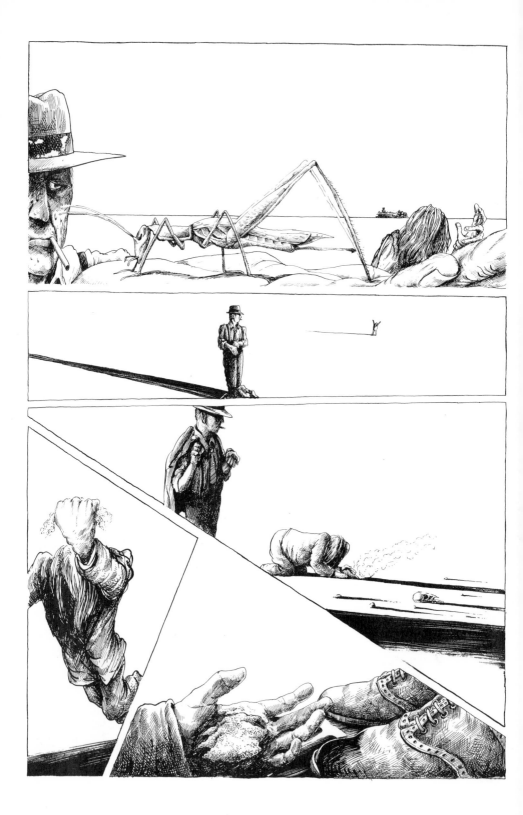

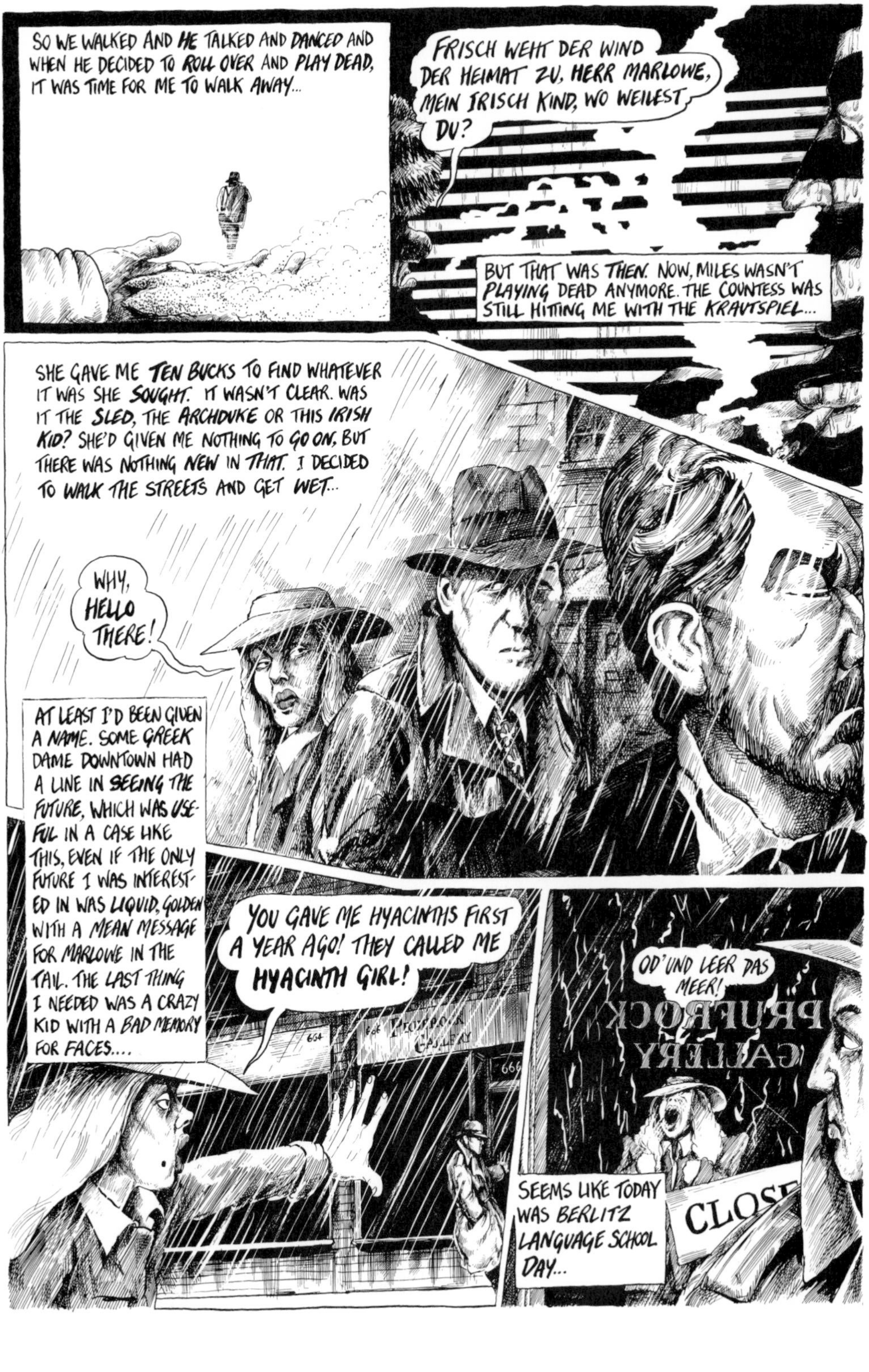

SO WE WALKED AND HE TALKED AND DANCED AND WHEN HE DECIDED TO ROLL OVER AND PLAY DEAD, IT WAS TIME FOR ME TO WALK AWAY...
FRISCH WEHT DER WIND DER HEIMAT ZU, HERR MARLOWE, MEIN IRISCH KIND, WO WEILEST DU?
BUT THAT WAS THEN. NOW, MILES WASN'T PLAYING DEAD ANYMORE. THE COUNTESS WAS STILL HITTING ME WITH THE KRAUTSPIEL...
SHE GAVE ME TEN BUCKS TO FIND WHATEVER IT WAS SHE SOUGHT. IT WASN'T CLEAR. WAS IT THE SLED, THE ARCHDUKE OR THIS IRISH KID? SHE'D GIVEN ME NOTHING TO GO ON, BUT THERE WAS NOTHING NEW IN THAT. I DECIDED TO WALK THE STREETS AND GET WET...
WHY, HELLO THERE!
AT LEAST I'D BEEN GIVEN A NAME. SOME GREEK DAME DOWNTOWN HAD A LINE IN SEEING THE FUTURE, WHICH WAS USEFUL IN A CASE LIKE THIS, EVEN IF THE ONLY FUTURE I WAS INTERESTED IN WAS LIQUID, GOLDEN WITH A MEAN MESSAGE FOR MARLOWE IN THE TAIL. THE LAST THING I NEEDED WAS A CRAZY KID WITH A BAD MEMORY FOR FACES....
YOU GAVE ME HYACINTHS FIRST A YEAR AGO! THEY CALLED ME HYACINTH GIRL!
OD' UND LEER DAS MEER!
PRUFROCK GALLERY
SEEMS LIKE TODAY WAS BERLITZ LANGUAGE SCHOOL DAY...
CLOSE

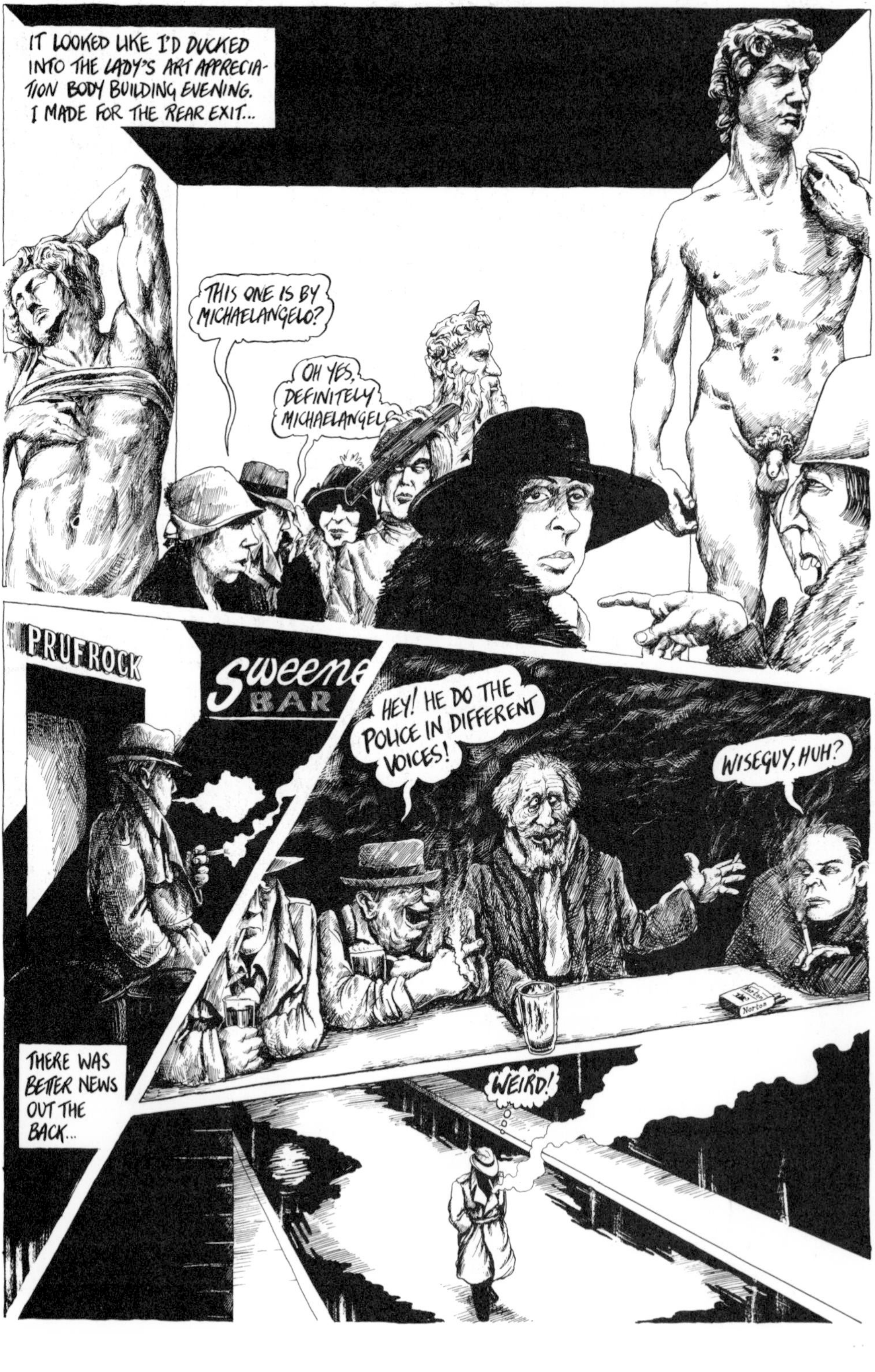
IT LOOKED LIKE I'D DUCKED INTO THE LADY'S ART APPRECIATION BODY BUILDING EVENING. I MADE FOR THE REAR EXIT...
THIS ONE IS BY MICHAELANGELO?
OH YES, DEFINITELY MICHAELANGELO
PRUFROCK
Sweene
BAR
HEY! HE DO THE POLICE IN DIFFERENT VOICES!
WISEGUY, HUH?
THERE WAS BETTER NEWS OUT THE BACK...
WEIRD!

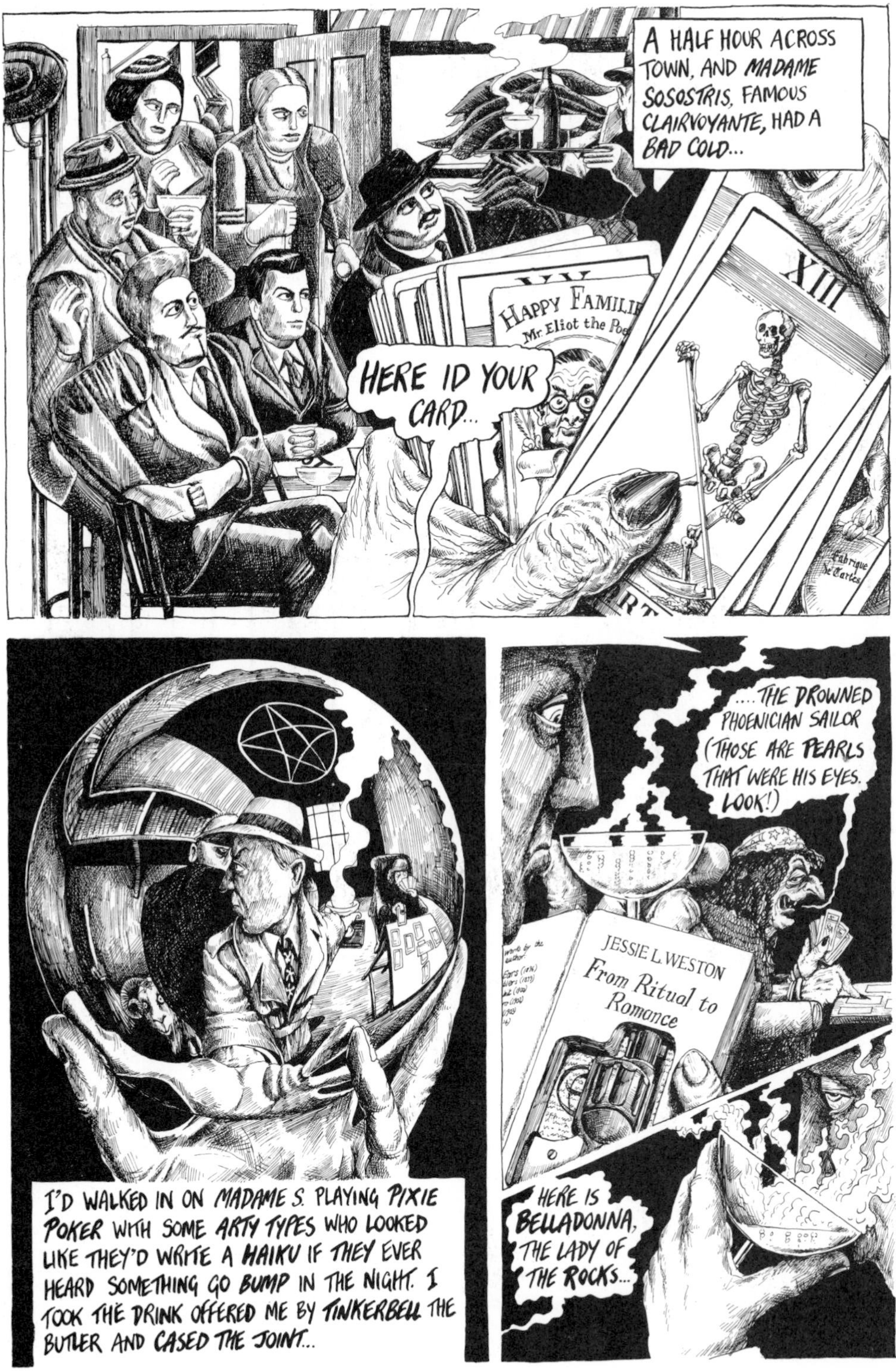

A HALF HOUR ACROSS TOWN, AND MADAME SOSOSTRIS, FAMOUS CLAIRVOYANTE, HAD A BAD COLD...
HERE ID YOUR CARD...
XIII
Fabrique de Cartes
I'D WALKED IN ON MADAME S. PLAYING PIXIE POKER WITH SOME ARTY TYPES WHO LOOKED LIKE THEY'D WRITE A HAIKU IF THEY EVER HEARD SOMETHING GO BUMP IN THE NIGHT. I TOOK THE DRINK OFFERED ME BY TINKERBELL THE BUTLER AND CASED THE JOINT...
....THE DROWNED PHOENICIAN SAILOR (THOSE ARE PEARLS THAT WERE HIS EYES. LOOK!)
JESSIE L. WESTON
From Ritual to Romance
HERE IS BELLADONNA, THE LADY OF THE ROCKS...

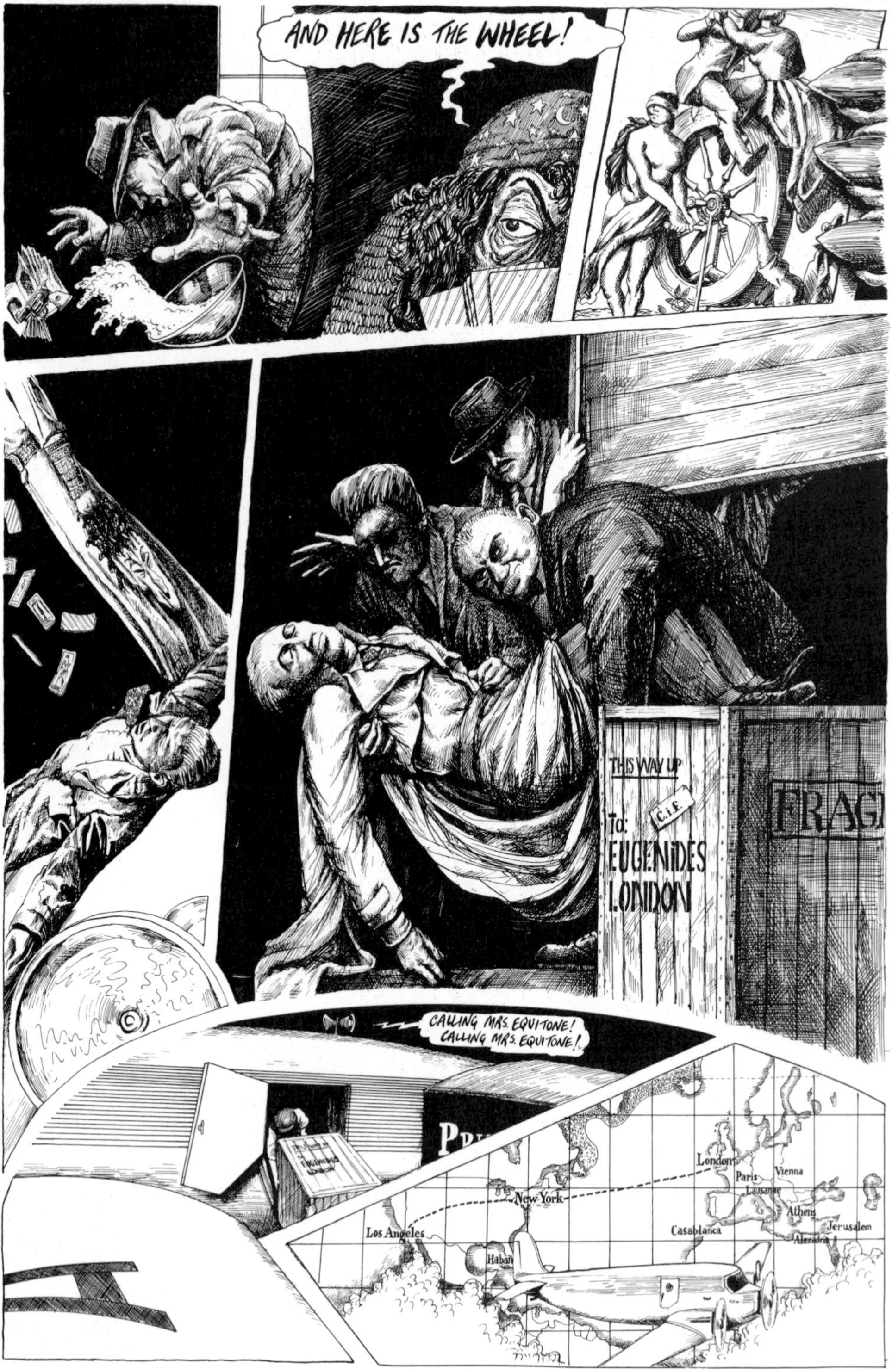
AND HERE IS THE WHEEL!
THIS WAY UP
C.i.F.
To:
EUGENIDES
LONDON
FRAG
CALLING MRS. EQUITONE!
CALLING MRS. EQUITONE!
PRI
London
Paris
Vienna
Lausanne
Athens
Jerusalem
Casablanca
New York
Los Angeles

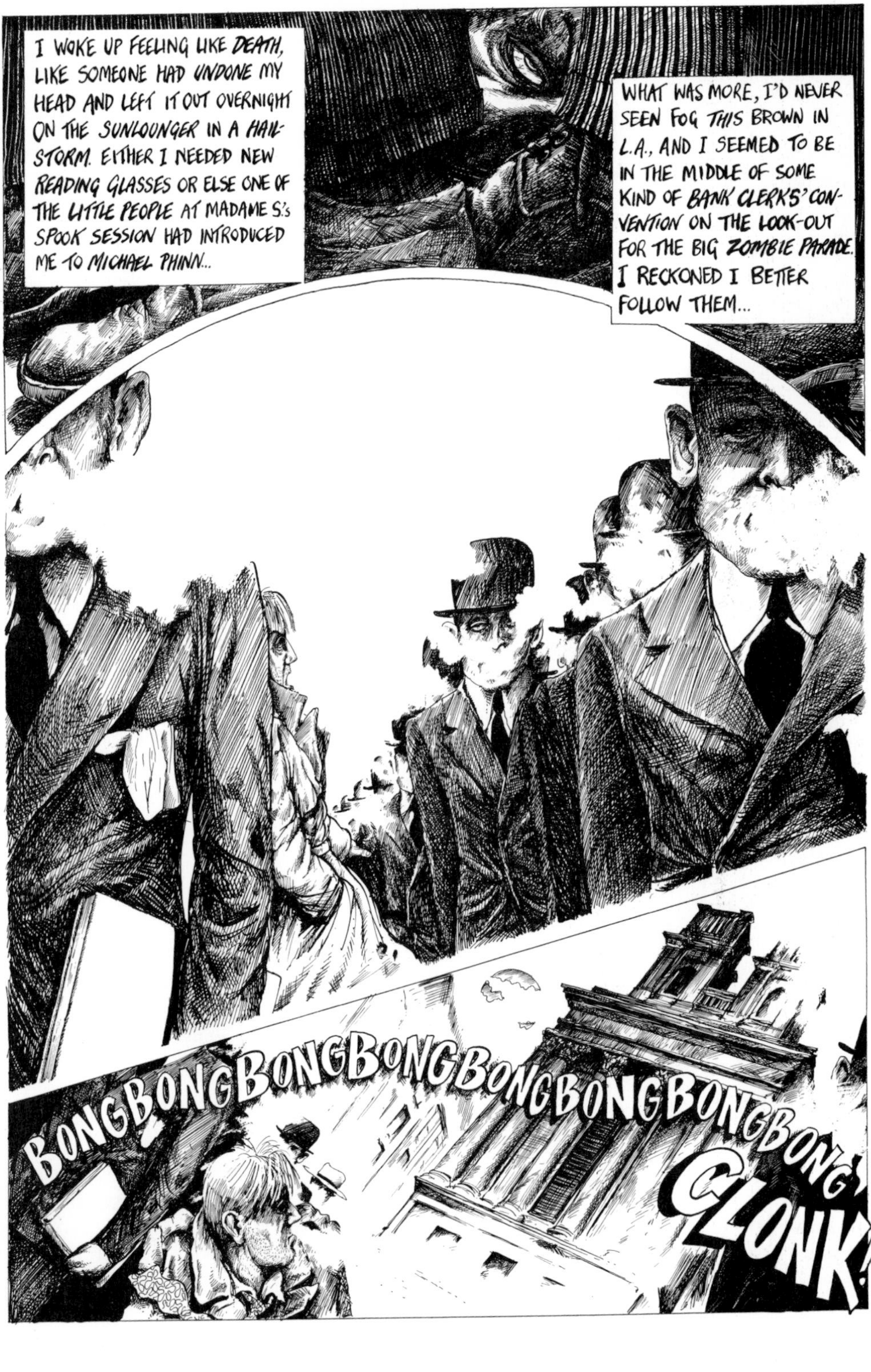
I WOKE UP FEELING LIKE DEATH, LIKE SOMEONE HAD UNDONE MY HEAD AND LEFT IT OUT OVERNIGHT ON THE SUNLOUNGER IN A HAIL-STORM. EITHER I NEEDED NEW READING GLASSES OR ELSE ONE OF THE LITTLE PEOPLE AT MADAME S.'s SPOOK SESSION HAD INTRODUCED ME TO MICHAEL PHINN...
WHAT WAS MORE, I'D NEVER SEEN FOG THIS BROWN IN L.A., AND I SEEMED TO BE IN THE MIDDLE OF SOME KIND OF BANK CLERK'S' CON-VENTION ON THE LOOK-OUT FOR THE BIG ZOMBIE PARADE. I RECKONED I BETTER FOLLOW THEM...
BONGBONGBONGBONGBONGBONGBONGBONGBONG
CLONK!

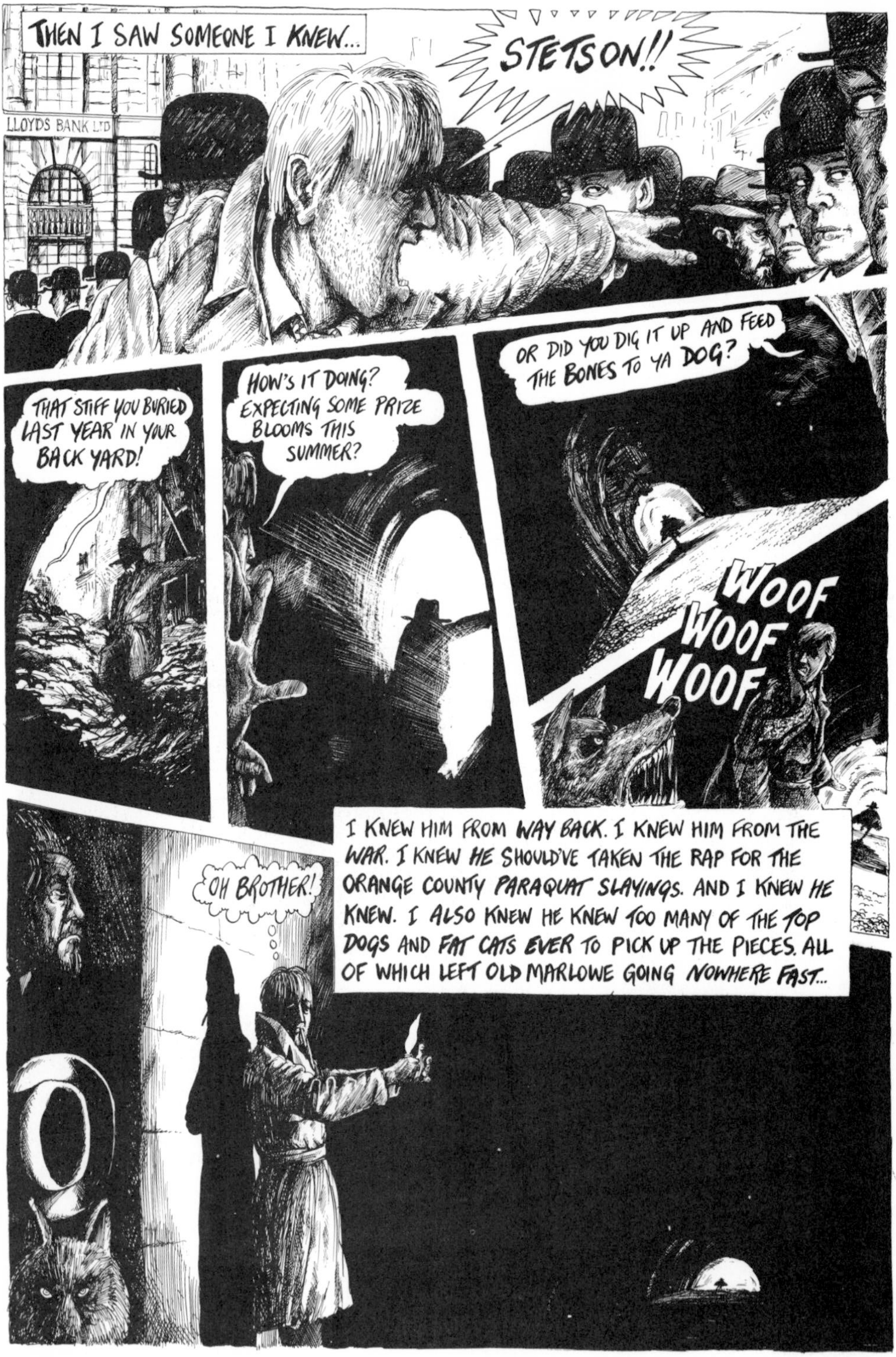
THEN I SAW SOMEONE I KNEW...
STETSON!!
LLOYDS BANK LTD
THAT STIFF YOU BURIED LAST YEAR IN YOUR BACK YARD!
HOW'S IT DOING? EXPECTING SOME PRIZE BLOOMS THIS SUMMER?
OR DID YOU DIG IT UP AND FEED THE BONES TO YA DOG?
WOOF WOOF WOOF
OH BROTHER!
I KNEW HIM FROM WAY BACK. I KNEW HIM FROM THE WAR. I KNEW HE SHOULD'VE TAKEN THE RAP FOR THE ORANGE COUNTY PARAQUAT SLAYINGS. AND I KNEW HE KNEW. I ALSO KNEW HE KNEW TOO MANY OF THE TOP DOGS AND FAT CATS EVER TO PICK UP THE PIECES. ALL OF WHICH LEFT OLD MARLOWE GOING NOWHERE FAST...

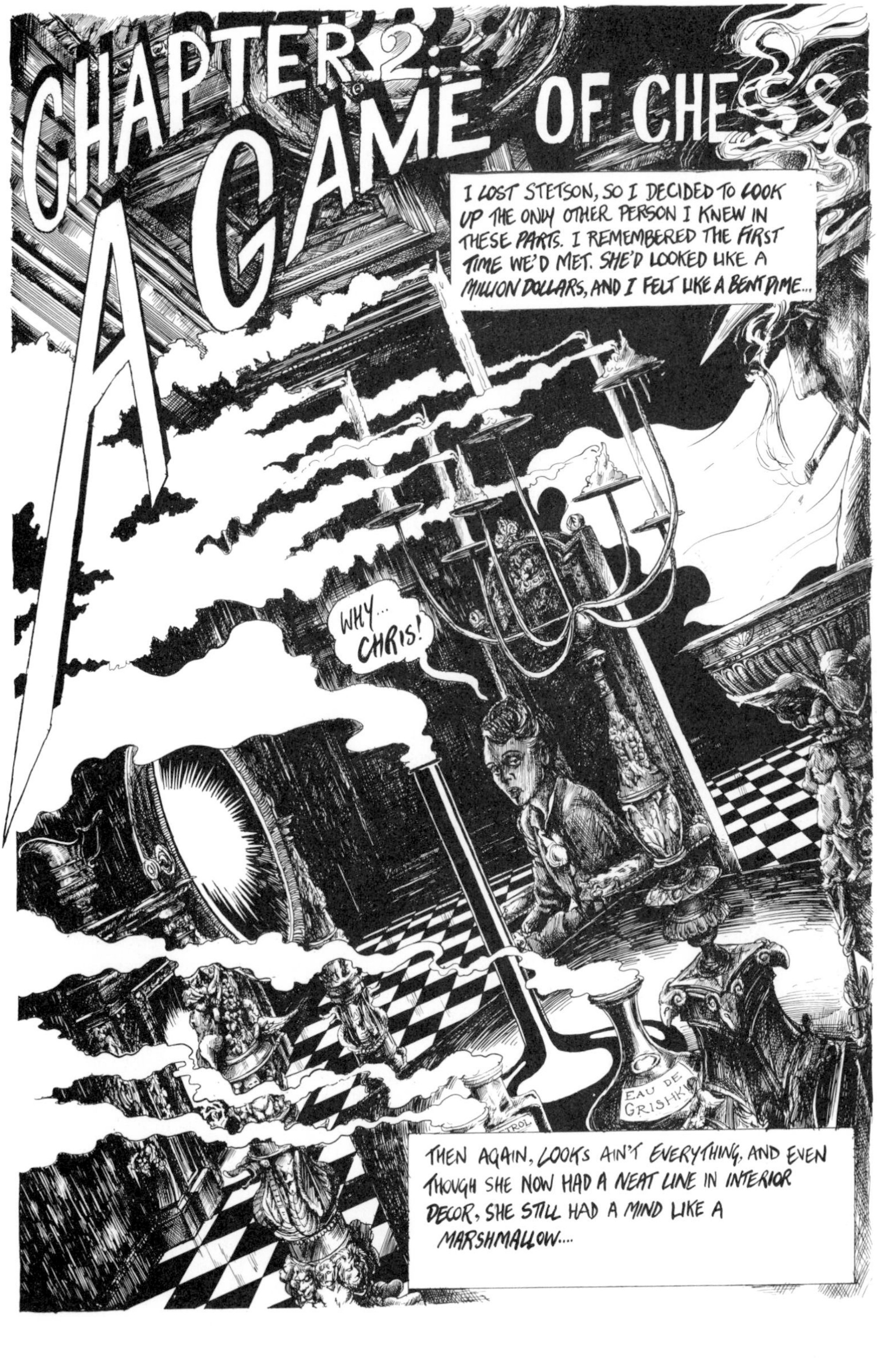
CHAPTER 2: A GAME OF CHESS
I LOST STETSON, SO I DECIDED TO LOOK UP THE ONLY OTHER PERSON I KNEW IN THESE PARTS. I REMEMBERED THE FIRST TIME WE'D MET. SHE'D LOOKED LIKE A MILLION DOLLARS, AND I FELT LIKE A BENT DIME...
WHY... CHRIS!
EAU DE GRISHKI
THEN AGAIN, LOOKS AIN'T EVERYTHING, AND EVEN THOUGH SHE NOW HAD A NEAT LINE IN INTERIOR DECOR, SHE STILL HAD A MIND LIKE A MARSHMALLOW....

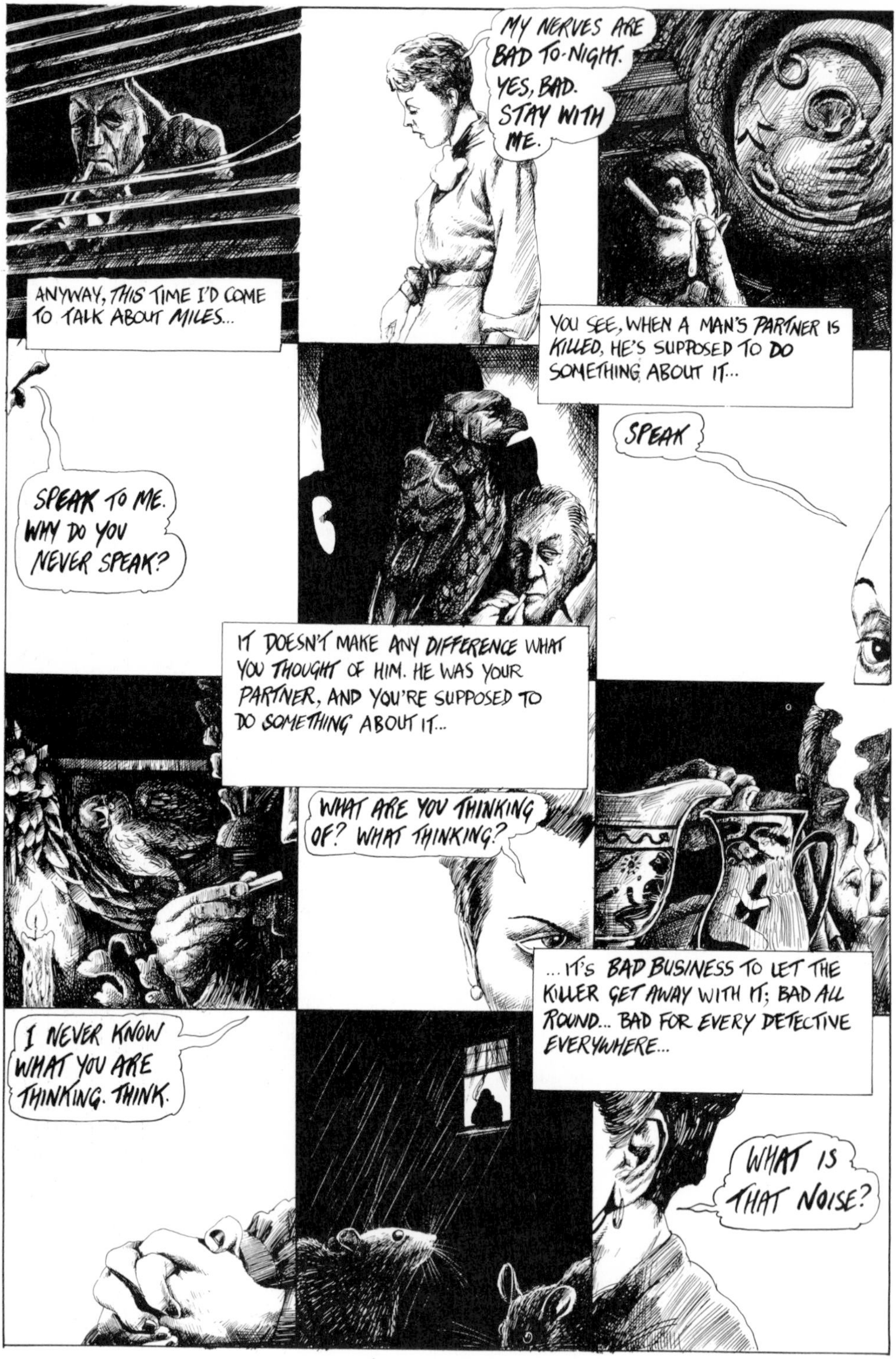

MY NERVES ARE BAD TO-NIGHT. YES, BAD. STAY WITH ME.
ANYWAY, THIS TIME I'D COME TO TALK ABOUT MILES...
YOU SEE, WHEN A MAN'S PARTNER IS KILLED, HE'S SUPPOSED TO DO SOMETHING ABOUT IT...
SPEAK TO ME. WHY DO YOU NEVER SPEAK?
SPEAK
IT DOESN'T MAKE ANY DIFFERENCE WHAT YOU THOUGHT OF HIM. HE WAS YOUR PARTNER, AND YOU'RE SUPPOSED TO DO SOMETHING ABOUT IT...
WHAT ARE YOU THINKING OF? WHAT THINKING?
...IT'S BAD BUSINESS TO LET THE KILLER GET AWAY WITH IT; BAD ALL ROUND... BAD FOR EVERY DETECTIVE EVERYWHERE...
I NEVER KNOW WHAT YOU ARE THINKING. THINK.
WHAT IS THAT NOISE?

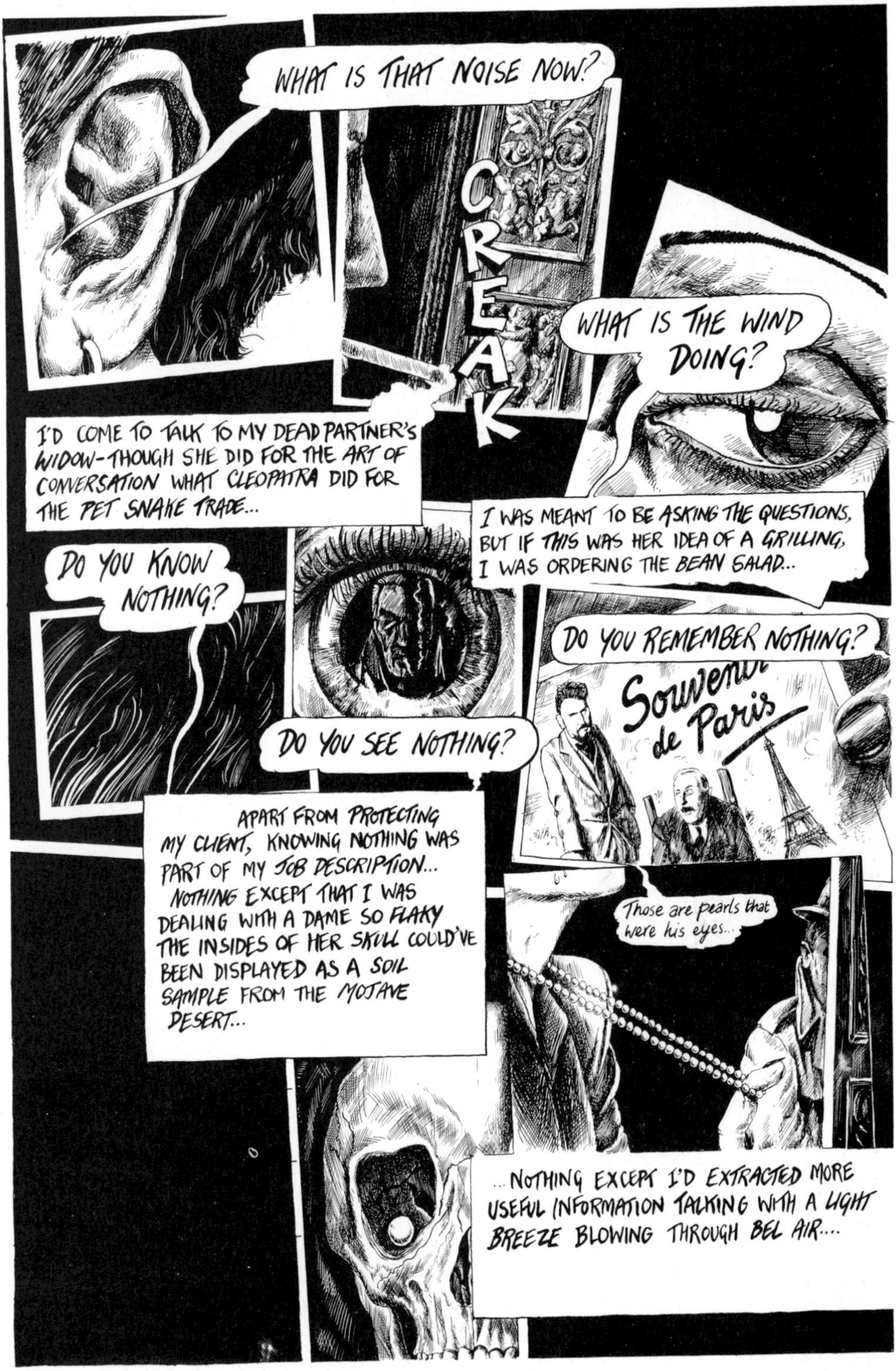
WHAT IS THAT NOISE NOW?
CREAK
WHAT IS THE WIND DOING?
I'D COME TO TALK TO MY DEAD PARTNER'S WIDOW—THOUGH SHE DID FOR THE ART OF CONVERSATION WHAT CLEOPATRA DID FOR THE PET SNAKE TRADE...
I WAS MEANT TO BE ASKING THE QUESTIONS, BUT IF THIS WAS HER IDEA OF A GRILLING, I WAS ORDERING THE BEAN SALAD...
DO YOU KNOW NOTHING?
DO YOU SEE NOTHING?
DO YOU REMEMBER NOTHING?
Souvenir de Paris
APART FROM PROTECTING MY CLIENT, KNOWING NOTHING WAS PART OF MY JOB DESCRIPTION... NOTHING EXCEPT THAT I WAS DEALING WITH A DAME SO FLAKY THE INSIDES OF HER SKULL COULD'VE BEEN DISPLAYED AS A SOIL SAMPLE FROM THE MOJAVE DESERT...
Those are pearls that were his eyes...
...NOTHING EXCEPT I'D EXTRACTED MORE USEFUL INFORMATION TALKING WITH A LIGHT BREEZE BLOWING THROUGH BEL AIR....

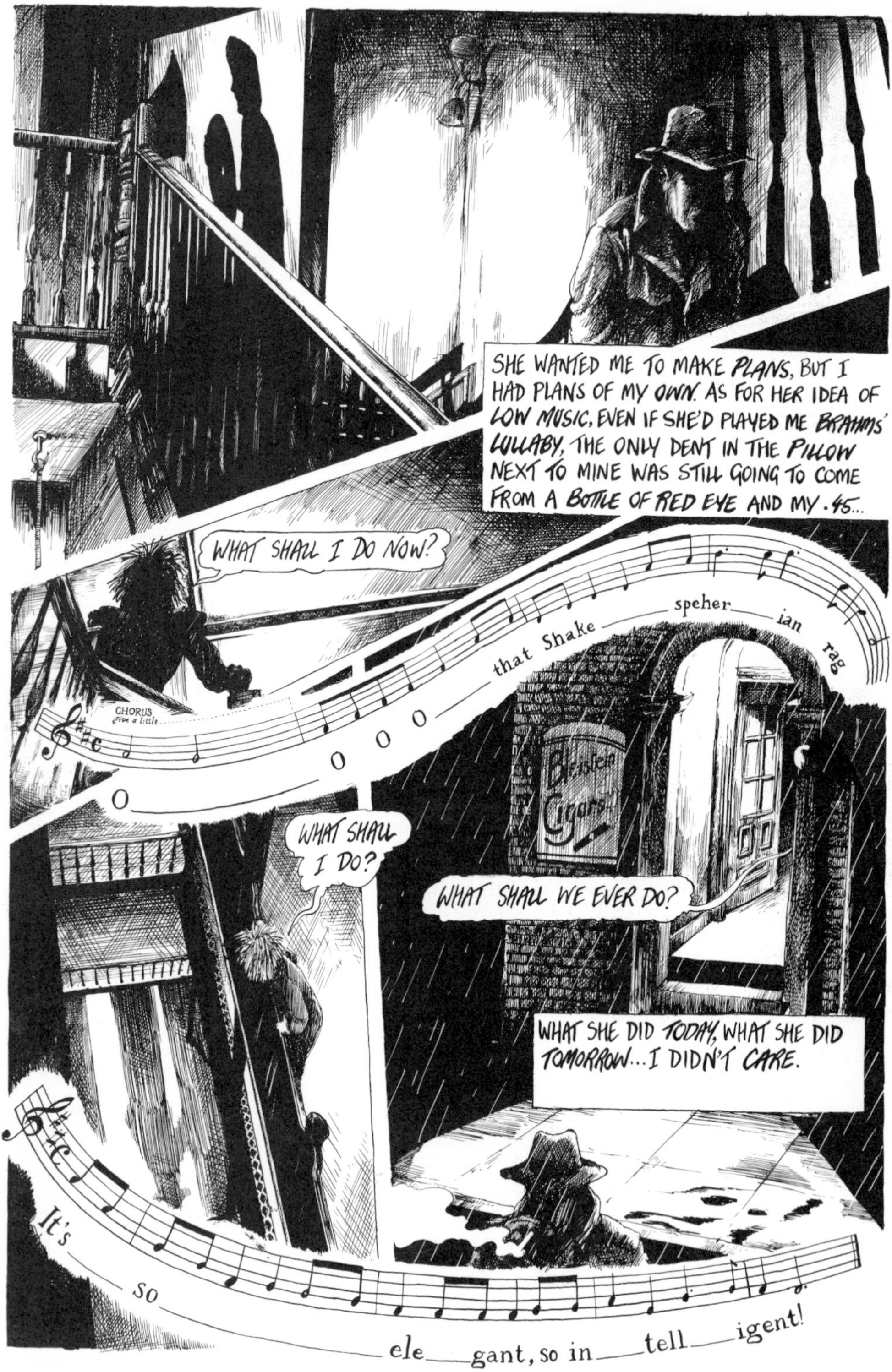
SHE WANTED ME TO MAKE PLANS, BUT I HAD PLANS OF MY OWN. AS FOR HER IDEA OF LOW MUSIC, EVEN IF SHE'D PLAYED ME BRAHMS' LULLABY, THE ONLY DENT IN THE PILLOW NEXT TO MINE WAS STILL GOING TO COME FROM A BOTTLE OF RED EYE AND MY .45...
WHAT SHALL I DO NOW?
CHORUS
give a little
O ___ O O O ___ that Shake ___ speher ___ ian rag
WHAT SHALL I DO?
WHAT SHALL WE EVER DO?
Bernstein Cigars
WHAT SHE DID TODAY, WHAT SHE DID TOMORROW... I DIDN'T CARE.
It's ___ so ___ ele ___ gant, so in ___ tell ___ igent!

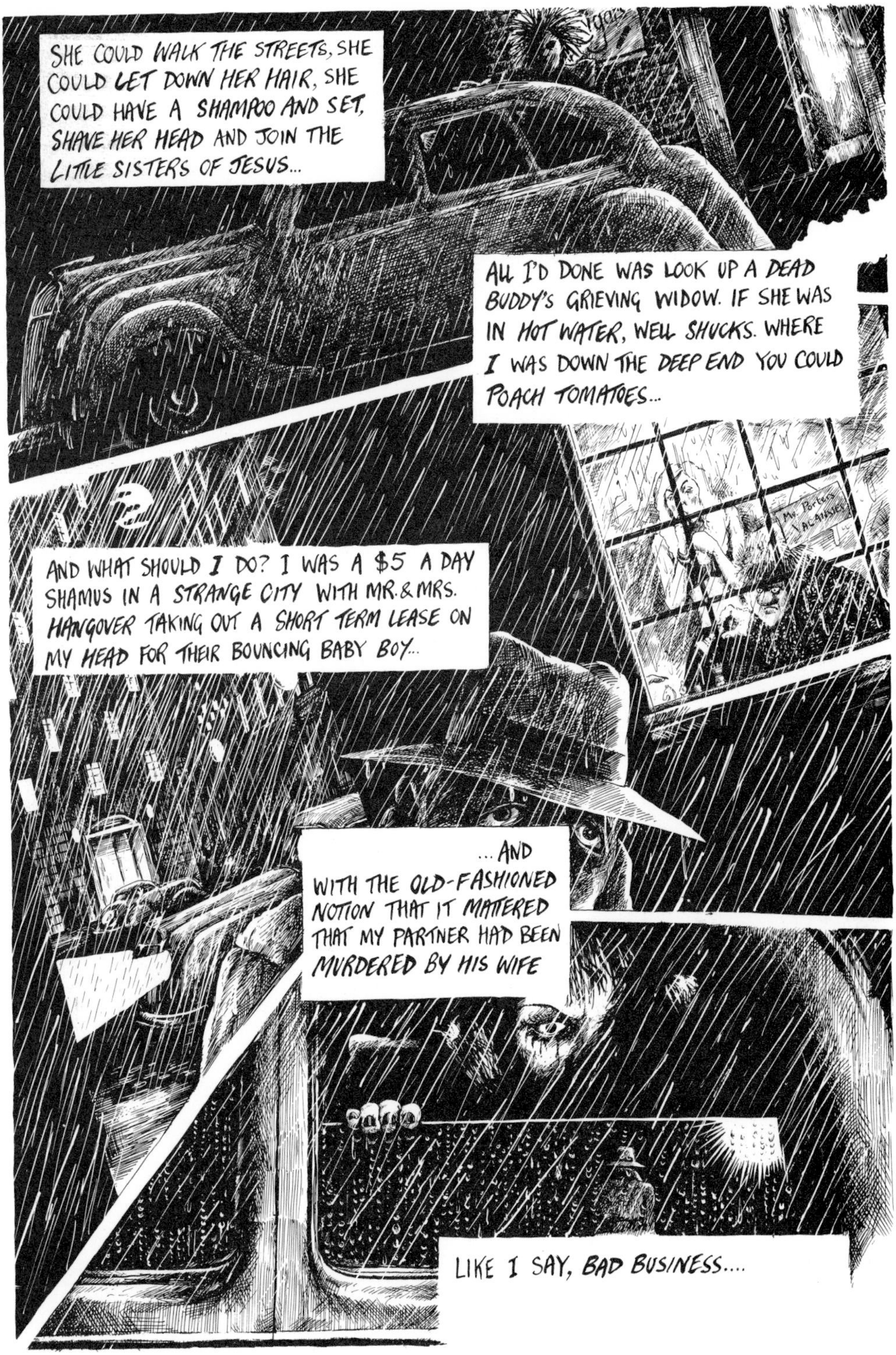
SHE COULD WALK THE STREETS, SHE COULD LET DOWN HER HAIR, SHE COULD HAVE A SHAMPOO AND SET, SHAVE HER HEAD AND JOIN THE LITTLE SISTERS OF JESUS...
ALL I'D DONE WAS LOOK UP A DEAD BUDDY'S GRIEVING WIDOW. IF SHE WAS IN HOT WATER, WELL SHUCKS. WHERE I WAS DOWN THE DEEP END YOU COULD POACH TOMATOES...
AND WHAT SHOULD I DO? I WAS A $5 A DAY SHAMUS IN A STRANGE CITY WITH MR. & MRS. HANGOVER TAKING OUT A SHORT TERM LEASE ON MY HEAD FOR THEIR BOUNCING BABY BOY...
...AND WITH THE OLD-FASHIONED NOTION THAT IT MATTERED THAT MY PARTNER HAD BEEN MURDERED BY HIS WIFE
LIKE I SAY, BAD BUSINESS....

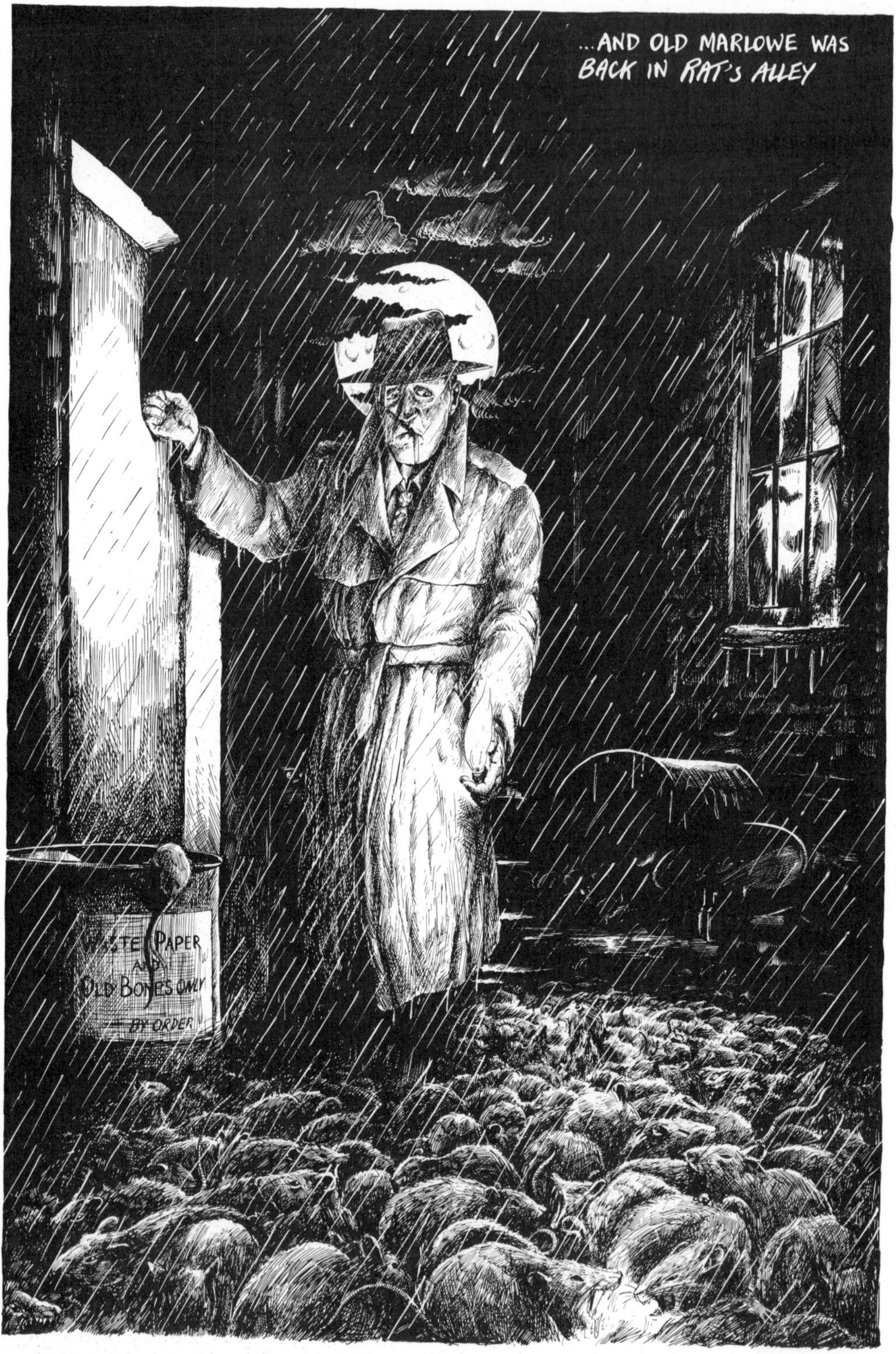
...AND OLD MARLOWE WAS
BACK IN RAT'S ALLEY
WASTE PAPER
AND
OLD BONES ONLY
— BY ORDER

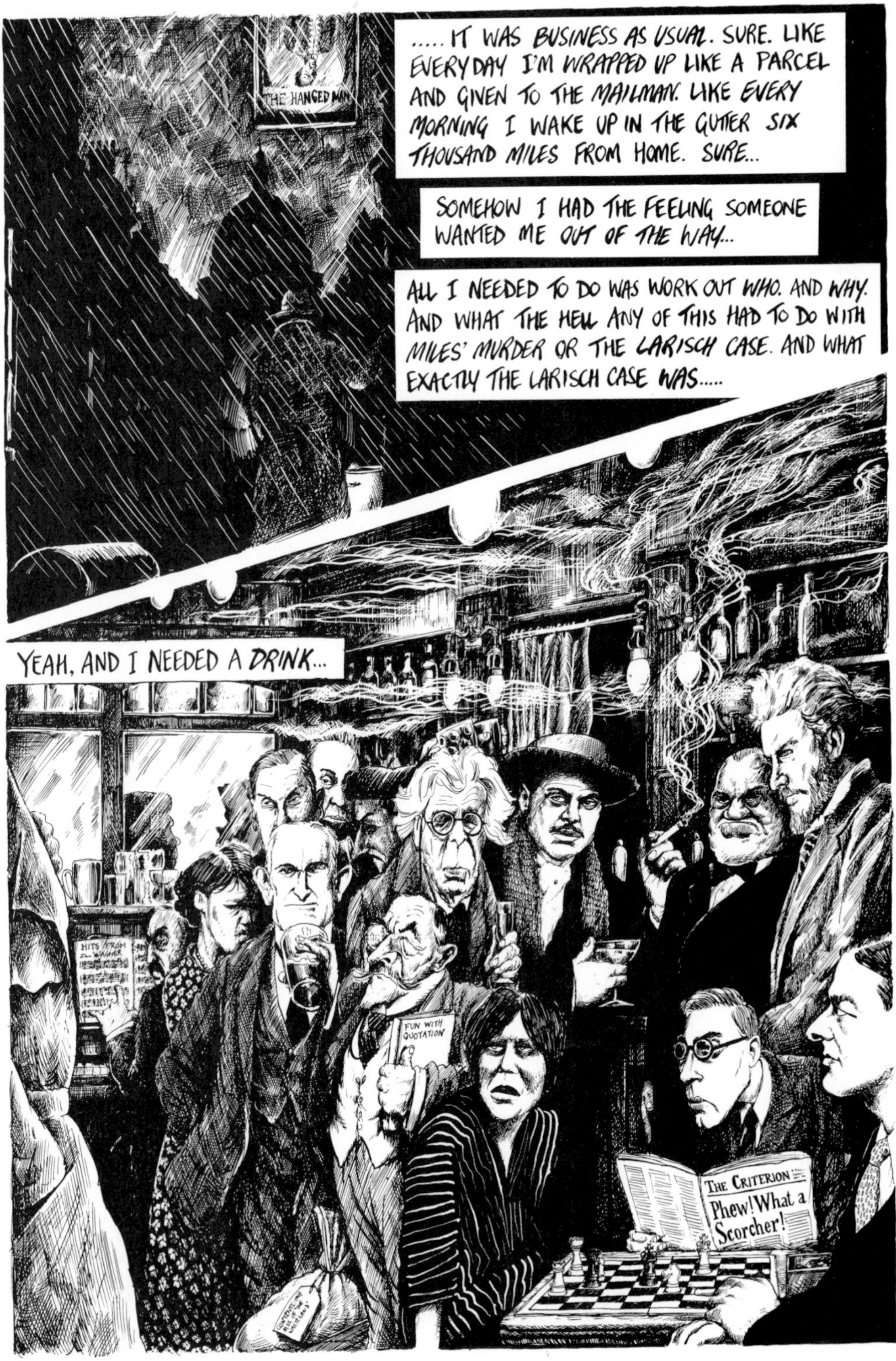
THE HANGED MAN
.....IT WAS BUSINESS AS USUAL. SURE. LIKE EVERYDAY I'M WRAPPED UP LIKE A PARCEL AND GIVEN TO THE MAILMAN. LIKE EVERY MORNING I WAKE UP IN THE GUTTER SIX THOUSAND MILES FROM HOME. SURE...
SOMEHOW I HAD THE FEELING SOMEONE WANTED ME OUT OF THE WAY...
ALL I NEEDED TO DO WAS WORK OUT WHO. AND WHY. AND WHAT THE HELL ANY OF THIS HAD TO DO WITH MILES' MURDER OR THE LARISCH CASE. AND WHAT EXACTLY THE LARISCH CASE WAS.....
YEAH, AND I NEEDED A DRINK...
FUN WITH QUOTATION
THE CRITERION
Phew! What a Scorcher!

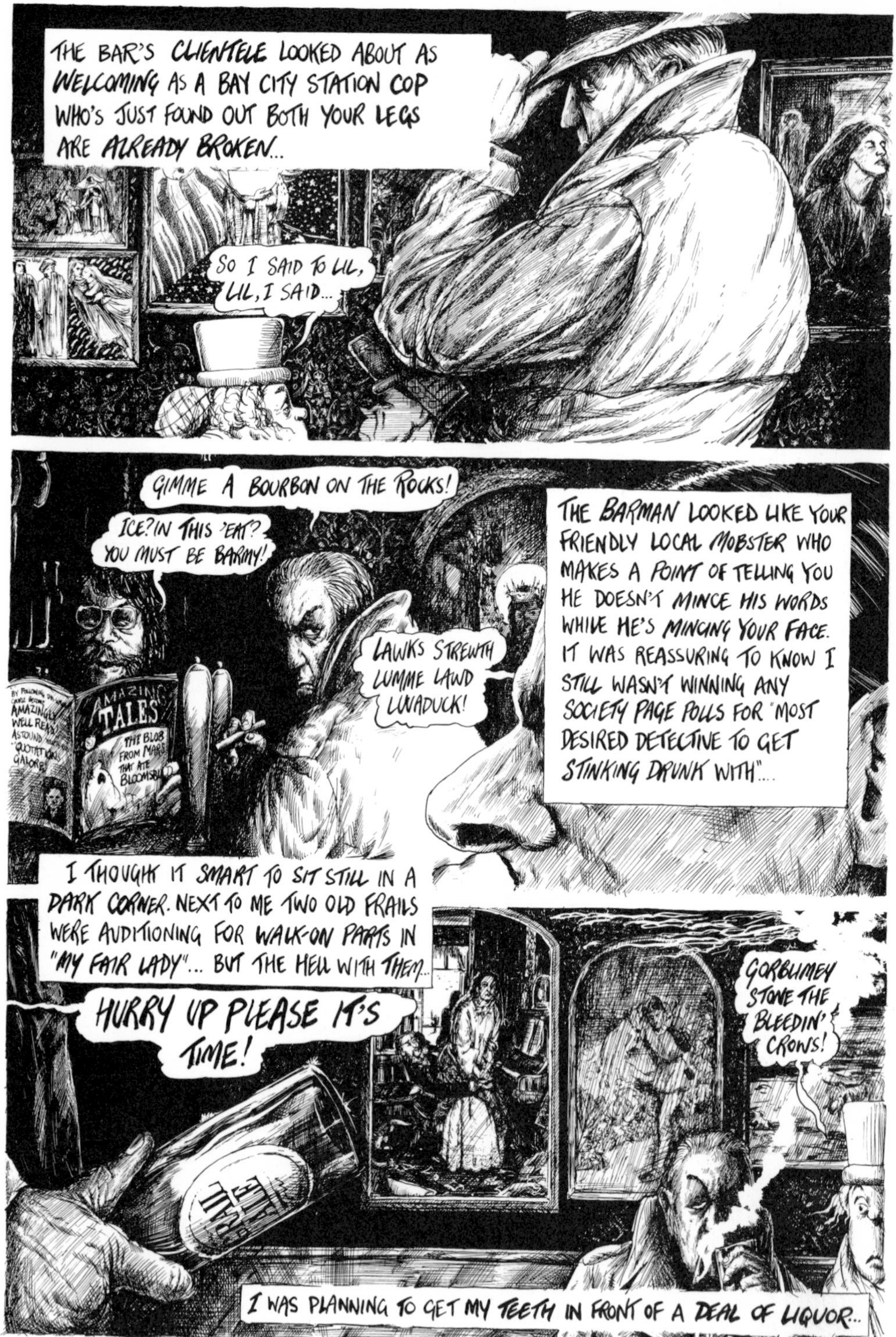
THE BAR'S CLIENTELE LOOKED ABOUT AS WELCOMING AS A BAY CITY STATION COP WHO'S JUST FOUND OUT BOTH YOUR LEGS ARE ALREADY BROKEN...
SO I SAID TO LIL, LIL, I SAID...
GIMME A BOURBON ON THE ROCKS!
ICE? IN THIS 'EAT? YOU MUST BE BARMY!
THE BARMAN LOOKED LIKE YOUR FRIENDLY LOCAL MOBSTER WHO MAKES A POINT OF TELLING YOU HE DOESN'T MINCE HIS WORDS WHILE HE'S MINCING YOUR FACE. IT WAS REASSURING TO KNOW I STILL WASN'T WINNING ANY SOCIETY PAGE POLLS FOR "MOST DESIRED DETECTIVE TO GET STINKING DRUNK WITH"....
LAWKS STREWTH LUMME LAWD LUVADUCK!
AMAZING TALES
I THOUGHT IT SMART TO SIT STILL IN A DARK CORNER. NEXT TO ME TWO OLD FRAILS WERE AUDITIONING FOR WALK-ON PARTS IN "MY FAIR LADY"... BUT THE HELL WITH THEM...
HURRY UP PLEASE IT'S TIME!
GORBLIMEY STONE THE BLEEDIN' CROWS!
I WAS PLANNING TO GET MY TEETH IN FRONT OF A DEAL OF LIQUOR...

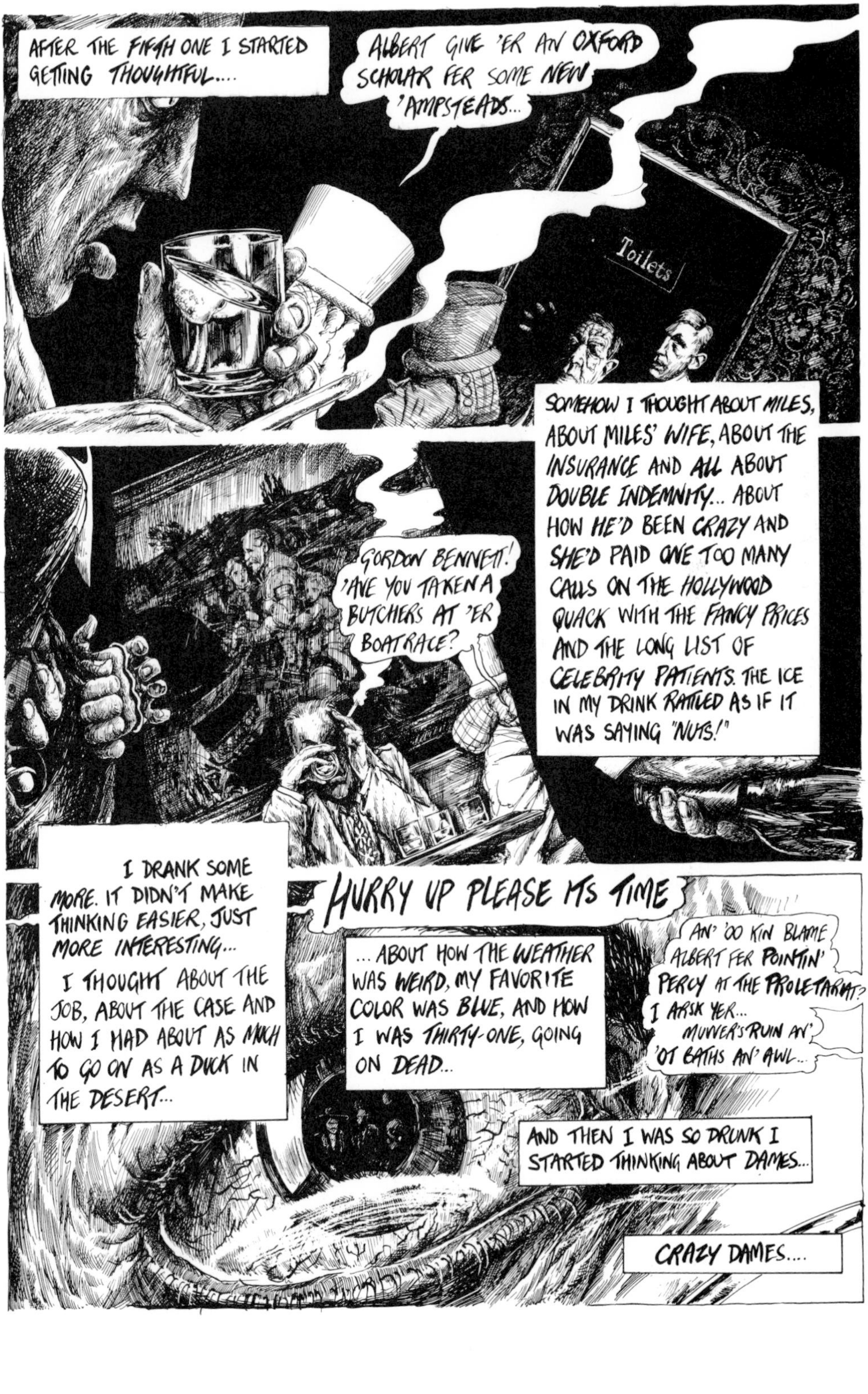

AFTER THE FIFTH ONE I STARTED GETTING THOUGHTFUL....
ALBERT GIVE 'ER AN OXFORD SCHOLAR FER SOME NEW 'AMPSTEADS...
Toilets
SOMEHOW I THOUGHT ABOUT MILES, ABOUT MILES' WIFE, ABOUT THE INSURANCE AND ALL ABOUT DOUBLE INDEMNITY... ABOUT HOW HE'D BEEN CRAZY AND SHE'D PAID ONE TOO MANY CALLS ON THE HOLLYWOOD QUACK WITH THE FANCY PRICES AND THE LONG LIST OF CELEBRITY PATIENTS. THE ICE IN MY DRINK RATTLED AS IF IT WAS SAYING "NUTS!"
GORDON BENNETT! 'AVE YOU TAKEN A BUTCHERS AT 'ER BOATRACE?
I DRANK SOME MORE. IT DIDN'T MAKE THINKING EASIER, JUST MORE INTERESTING...
I THOUGHT ABOUT THE JOB, ABOUT THE CASE AND HOW I HAD ABOUT AS MUCH TO GO ON AS A DUCK IN THE DESERT...
HURRY UP PLEASE ITS TIME
... ABOUT HOW THE WEATHER WAS WEIRD, MY FAVORITE COLOR WAS BLUE, AND HOW I WAS THIRTY-ONE, GOING ON DEAD...
AN' 'OO KIN BLAME ALBERT FER POINTIN' PERCY AT THE PROLETARIAT? I ARSK YER... MUVVER'S RUIN AN' 'OT BATHS AN' AWL...
AND THEN I WAS SO DRUNK I STARTED THINKING ABOUT DAMES...
CRAZY DAMES....

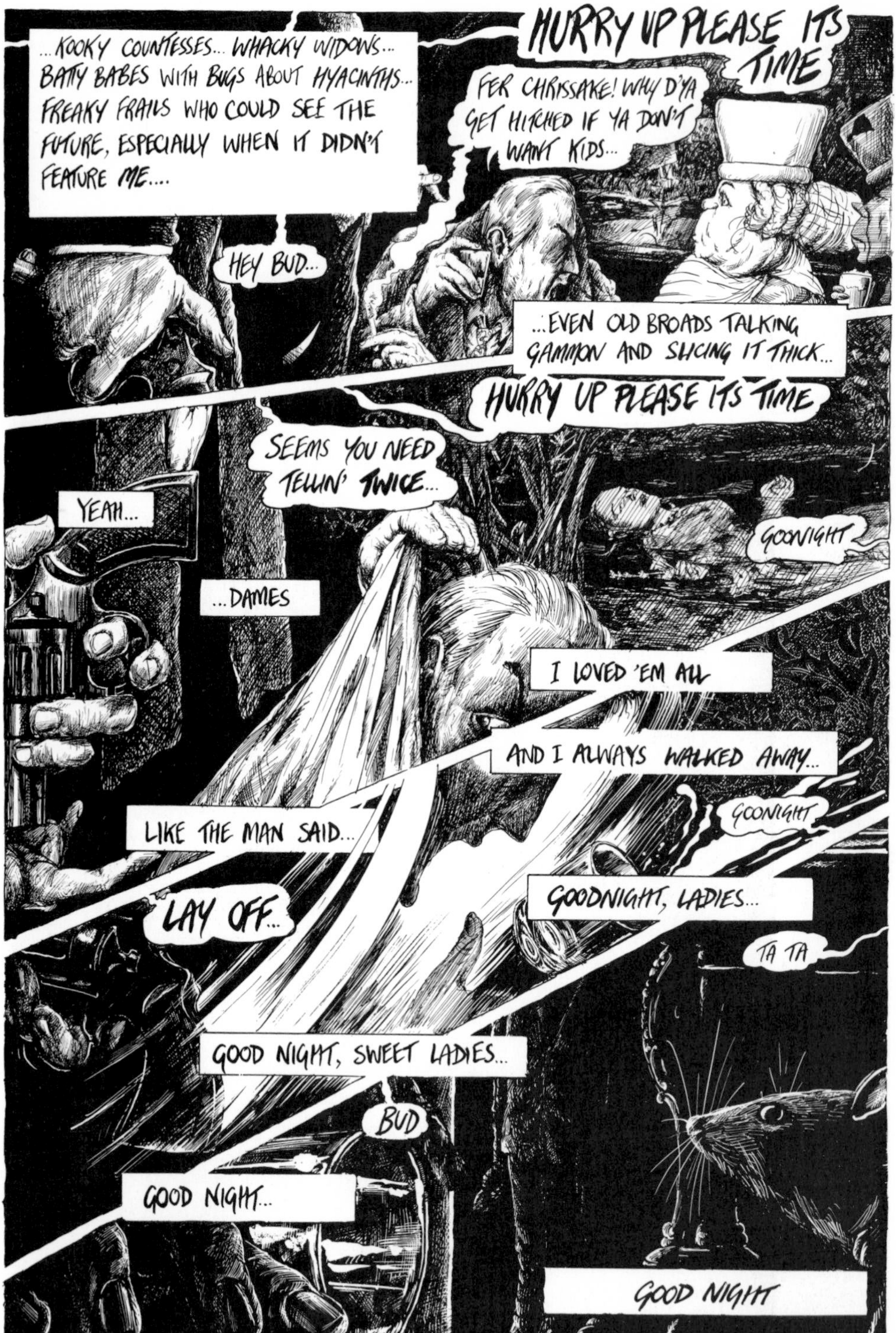

...KOOKY COUNTESSES... WHACKY WIDOWS... BATTY BABES WITH BUGS ABOUT HYACINTHS... FREAKY FRAILS WHO COULD SEE THE FUTURE, ESPECIALLY WHEN IT DIDN'T FEATURE ME....
HURRY UP PLEASE ITS TIME
FER CHRISSAKE! WHY D'YA GET HITCHED IF YA DON'T WANT KIDS...
HEY BUD...
...EVEN OLD BROADS TALKING GAMMON AND SLICING IT THICK...
HURRY UP PLEASE ITS TIME
SEEMS YOU NEED TELLIN' TWICE...
YEAH...
GOONIGHT
...DAMES
I LOVED 'EM ALL
AND I ALWAYS WALKED AWAY...
GOONIGHT
LIKE THE MAN SAID...
GOODNIGHT, LADIES...
LAY OFF...
TA TA
GOOD NIGHT, SWEET LADIES...
BUD
GOOD NIGHT...
GOOD NIGHT

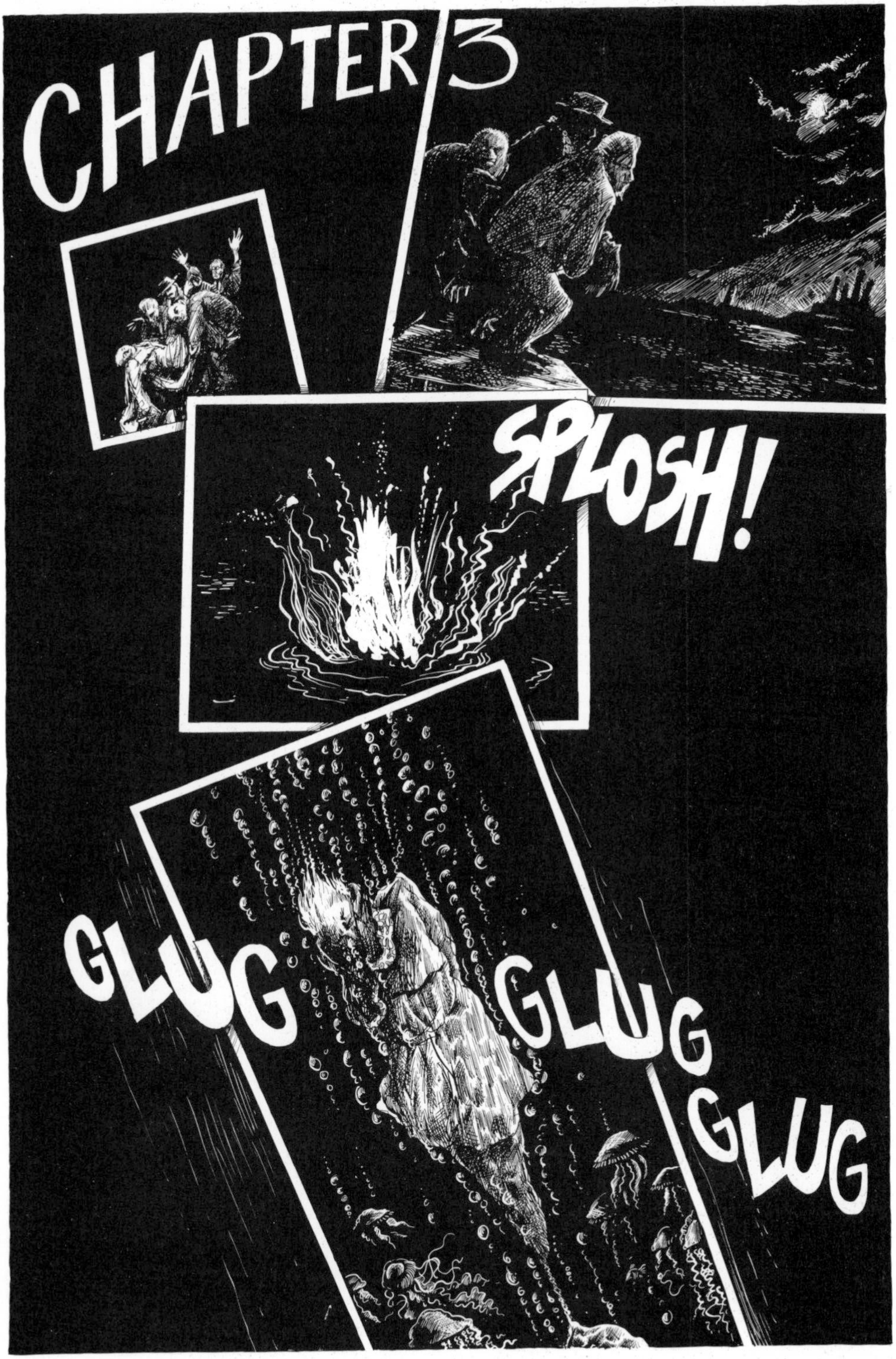
CHAPTER 3
SPLOSH!
GLUG
GLUG
GLUG

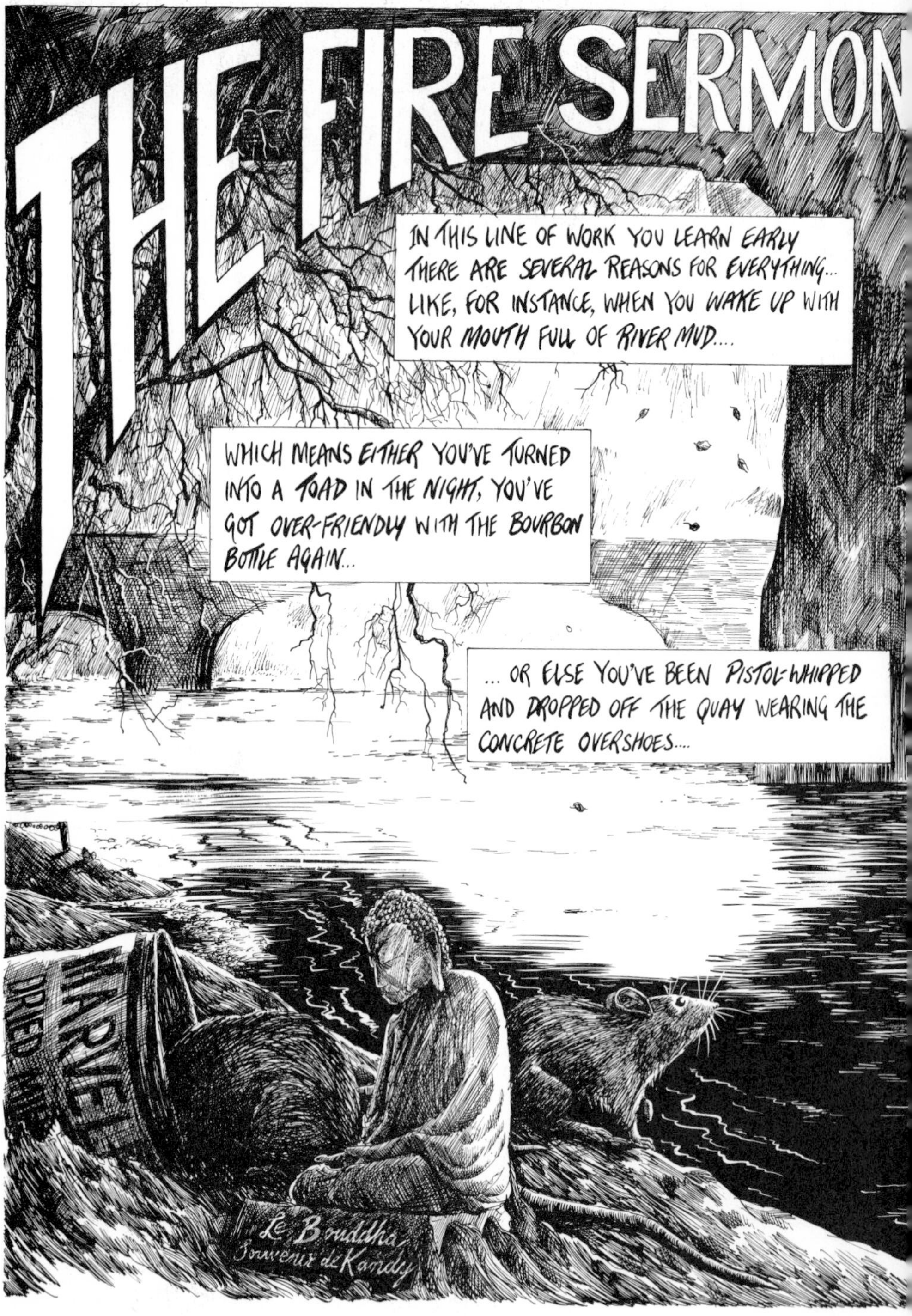
THE FIRE SERMON
IN THIS LINE OF WORK YOU LEARN EARLY THERE ARE SEVERAL REASONS FOR EVERYTHING... LIKE, FOR INSTANCE, WHEN YOU WAKE UP WITH YOUR MOUTH FULL OF RIVER MUD....
WHICH MEANS EITHER YOU'VE TURNED INTO A TOAD IN THE NIGHT, YOU'VE GOT OVER-FRIENDLY WITH THE BOURBON BOTTLE AGAIN...
... OR ELSE YOU'VE BEEN PISTOL-WHIPPED AND DROPPED OFF THE QUAY WEARING THE CONCRETE OVERSHOES....
Le Bouddha, Souvenir de Kandy

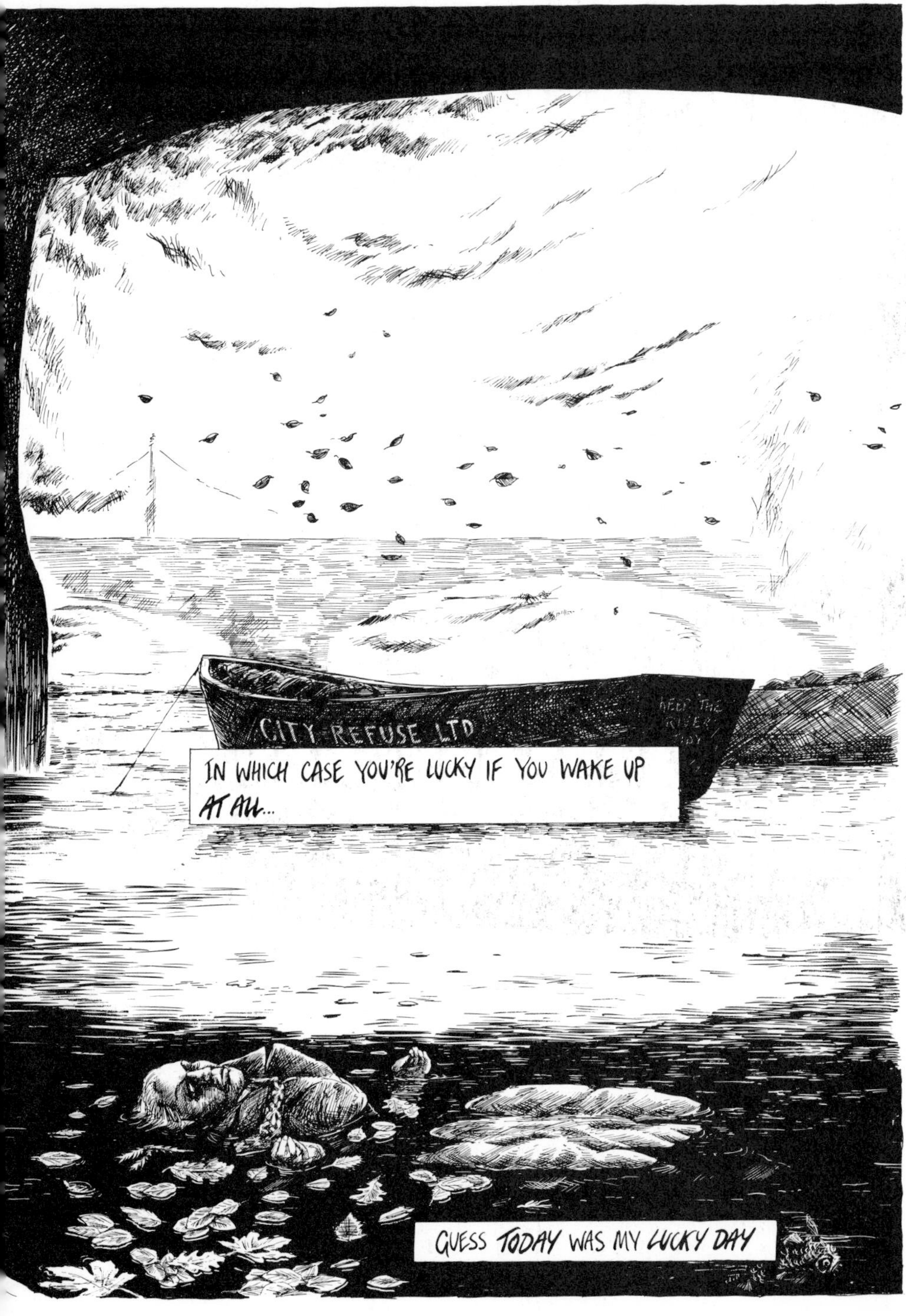
CITY REFUSE LTD
IN WHICH CASE YOU'RE LUCKY IF YOU WAKE UP AT ALL...
GUESS TODAY WAS MY LUCKY DAY

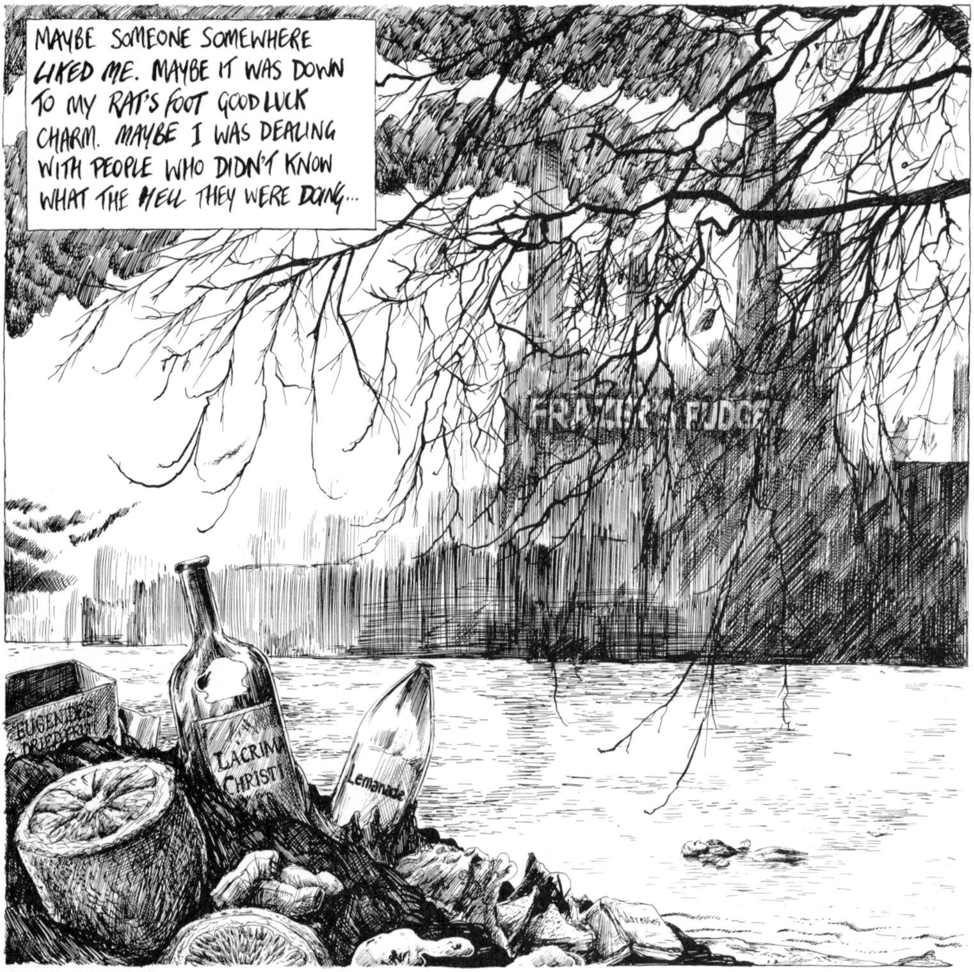
MAYBE SOMEONE SOMEWHERE LIKED ME. MAYBE IT WAS DOWN TO MY RAT'S FOOT GOOD LUCK CHARM. MAYBE I WAS DEALING WITH PEOPLE WHO DIDN'T KNOW WHAT THE HELL THEY WERE DOING...
LACRIMA CHRISTI
Lemanade

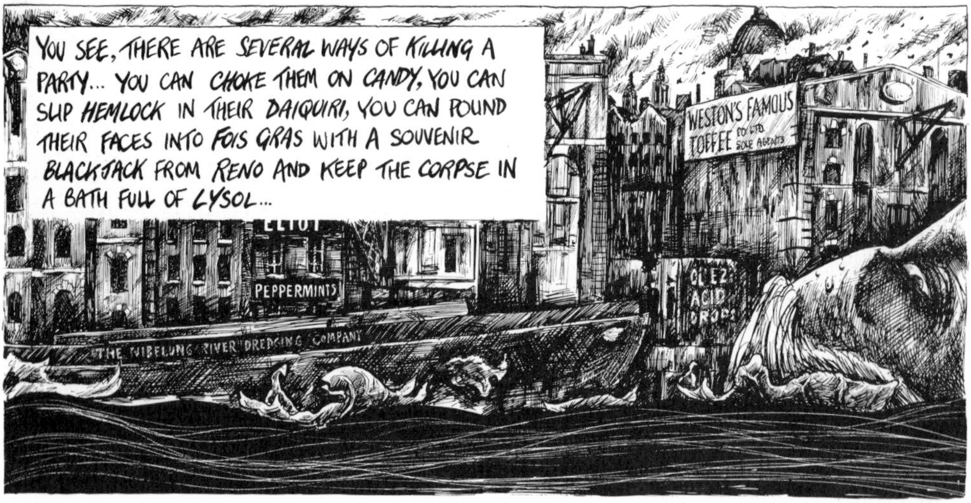
YOU SEE, THERE ARE SEVERAL WAYS OF KILLING A PARTY... YOU CAN CHOKE THEM ON CANDY, YOU CAN SLIP HEMLOCK IN THEIR DAIQUIRI, YOU CAN POUND THEIR FACES INTO FOIS GRAS WITH A SOUVENIR BLACKJACK FROM RENO AND KEEP THE CORPSE IN A BATH FULL OF LYSOL...
WESTON'S FAMOUS TOFFEE
SOLE AGENTS
PEPPERMINTS
ACID DROPS
THE NIBELUNG RIVER DREDGING COMPANY

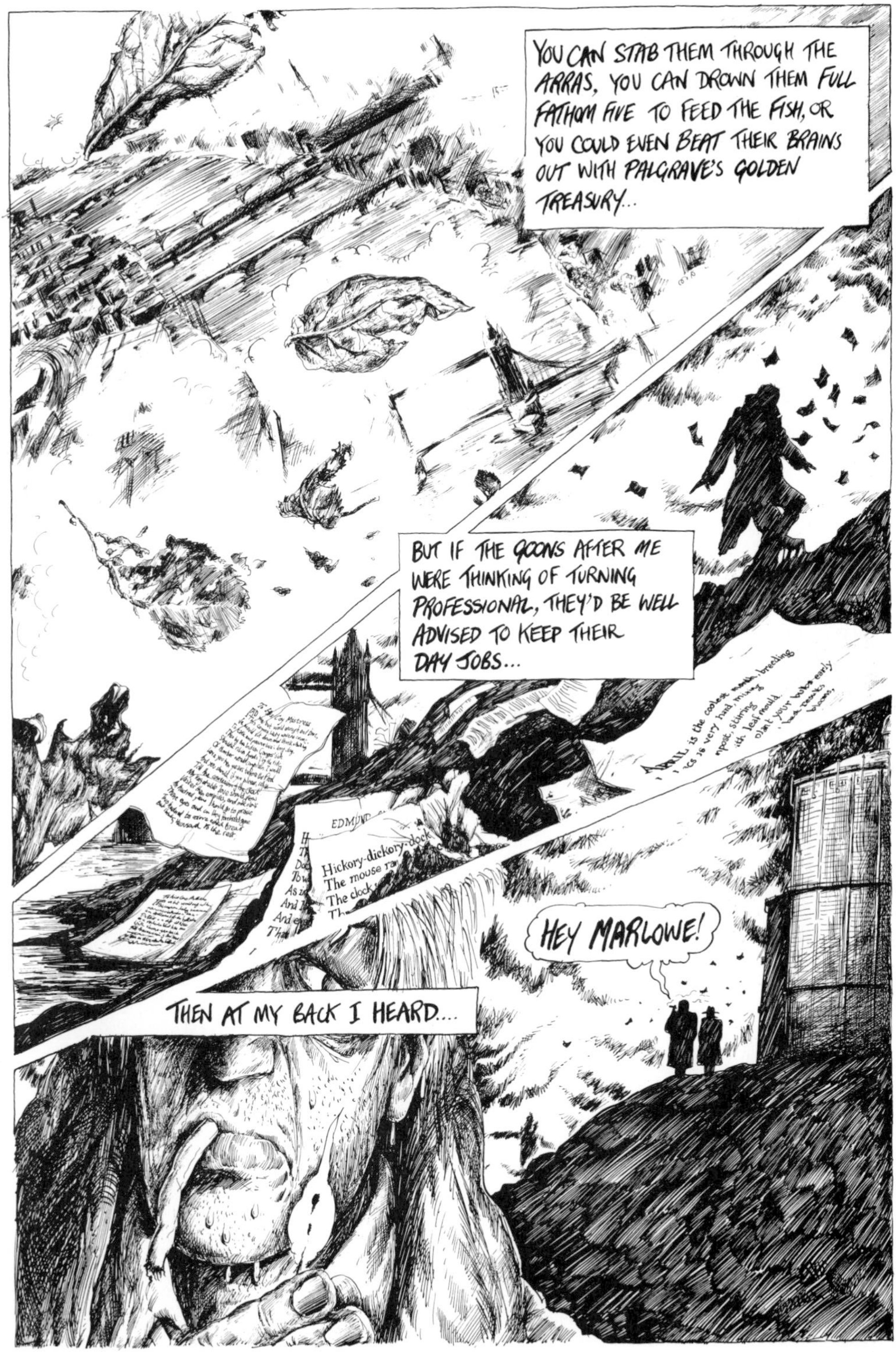
YOU CAN STAB THEM THROUGH THE ARRAS, YOU CAN DROWN THEM FULL FATHOM FIVE TO FEED THE FISH, OR YOU COULD EVEN BEAT THEIR BRAINS OUT WITH PALGRAVE'S GOLDEN TREASURY...
BUT IF THE GOONS AFTER ME WERE THINKING OF TURNING PROFESSIONAL, THEY'D BE WELL ADVISED TO KEEP THEIR DAY JOBS...
Hickory-dickory-dock
THEN AT MY BACK I HEARD...
HEY MARLOWE!

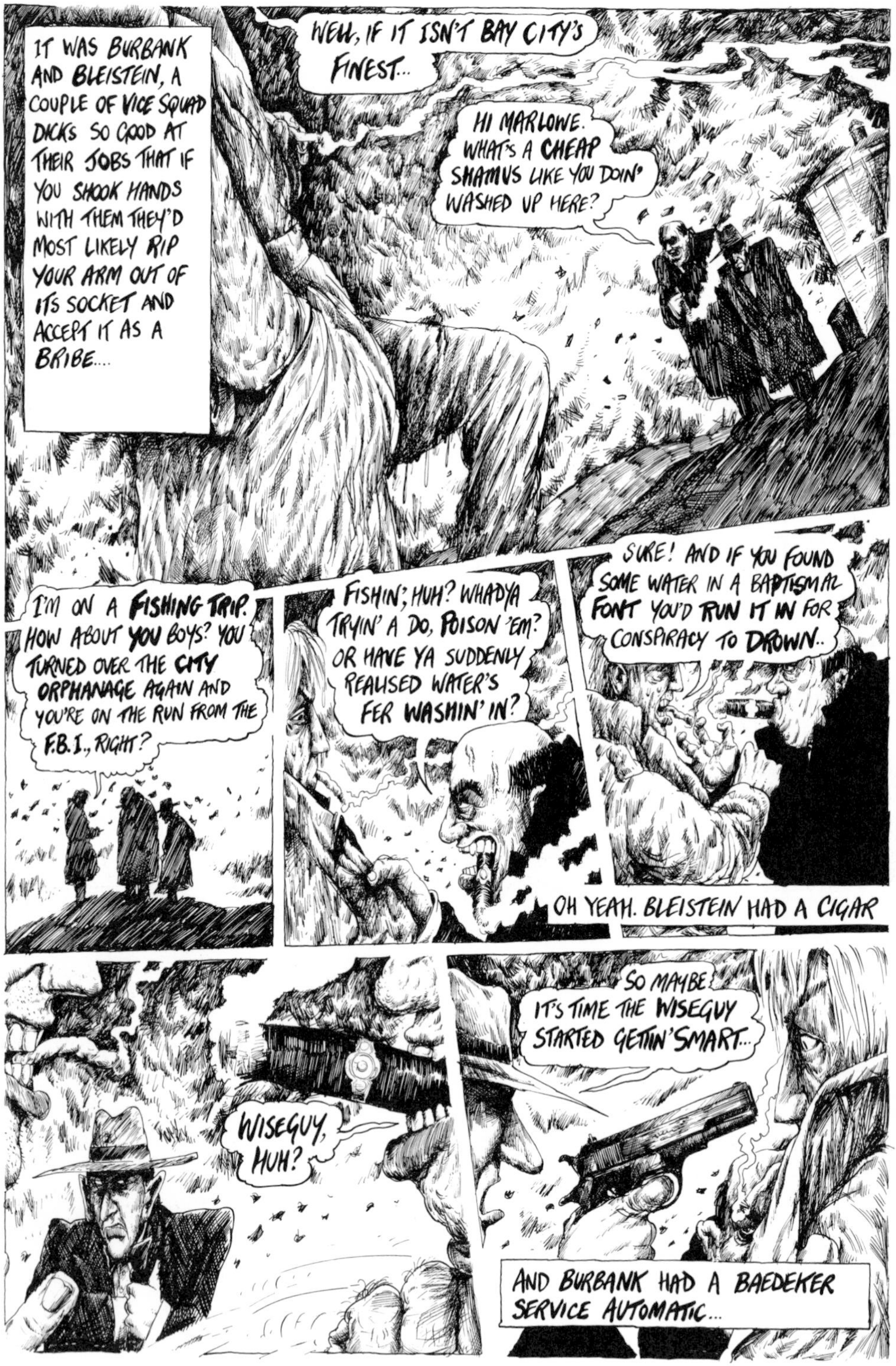
IT WAS BURBANK AND BLEISTEIN, A COUPLE OF VICE SQUAD DICKS SO GOOD AT THEIR JOBS THAT IF YOU SHOOK HANDS WITH THEM THEY'D MOST LIKELY RIP YOUR ARM OUT OF ITS SOCKET AND ACCEPT IT AS A BRIBE...
WELL, IF IT ISN'T BAY CITY'S FINEST...
HI MARLOWE. WHAT'S A CHEAP SHAMUS LIKE YOU DOIN' WASHED UP HERE?
I'M ON A FISHING TRIP. HOW ABOUT YOU BOYS? YOU TURNED OVER THE CITY ORPHANAGE AGAIN AND YOU'RE ON THE RUN FROM THE F.B.I., RIGHT?
FISHIN', HUH? WHADYA TRYIN' A DO, POISON 'EM? OR HAVE YA SUDDENLY REALISED WATER'S FER WASHIN' IN?
SURE! AND IF YOU FOUND SOME WATER IN A BAPTISMAL FONT YOU'D RUN IT IN FOR CONSPIRACY TO DROWN..
OH YEAH. BLEISTEIN HAD A CIGAR
WISEGUY, HUH?
SO MAYBE IT'S TIME THE WISEGUY STARTED GETTIN' SMART...
AND BURBANK HAD A BAEDEKER SERVICE AUTOMATIC...

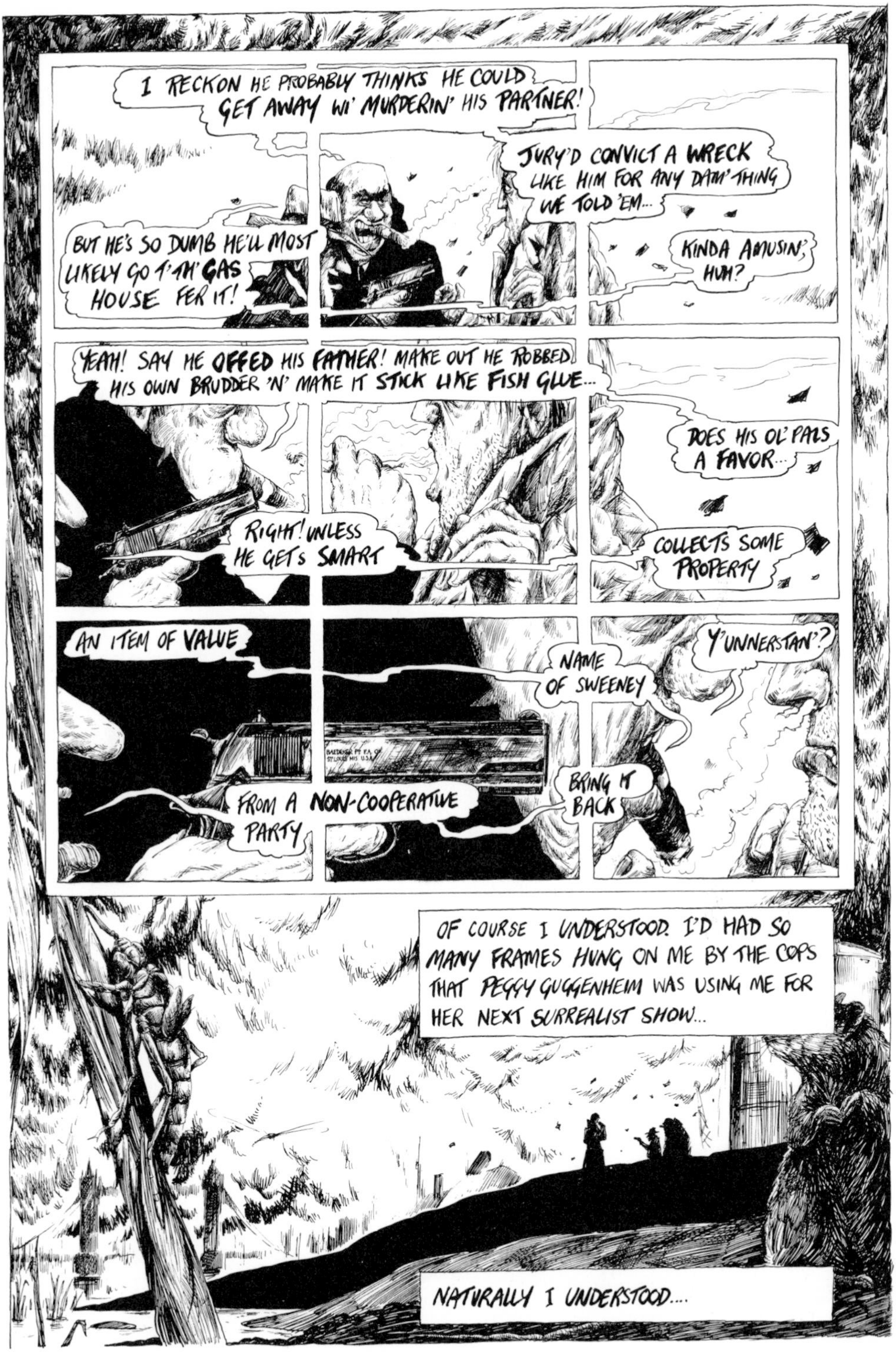
I RECKON HE PROBABLY THINKS HE COULD GET AWAY WI' MURDERIN' HIS PARTNER!
BUT HE'S SO DUMB HE'LL MOST LIKELY GO T' TH' GAS HOUSE FER IT!
JURY'D CONVICT A WRECK LIKE HIM FOR ANY DAM' THING WE TOLD 'EM...
KINDA AMUSIN', HUH?
YEAH! SAY HE OFFED HIS FATHER! MAKE OUT HE ROBBED HIS OWN BRUDDER 'N' MAKE IT STICK LIKE FISH GLUE...
DOES HIS OL' PALS A FAVOR...
RIGHT! UNLESS HE GETS SMART
COLLECTS SOME PROPERTY
AN ITEM OF VALUE
NAME OF SWEENEY
Y'UNNERSTAN'?
FROM A NON-COOPERATIVE PARTY
BRING IT BACK
OF COURSE I UNDERSTOOD. I'D HAD SO MANY FRAMES HUNG ON ME BY THE COPS THAT PEGGY GUGGENHEIM WAS USING ME FOR HER NEXT SURREALIST SHOW...
NATURALLY I UNDERSTOOD....

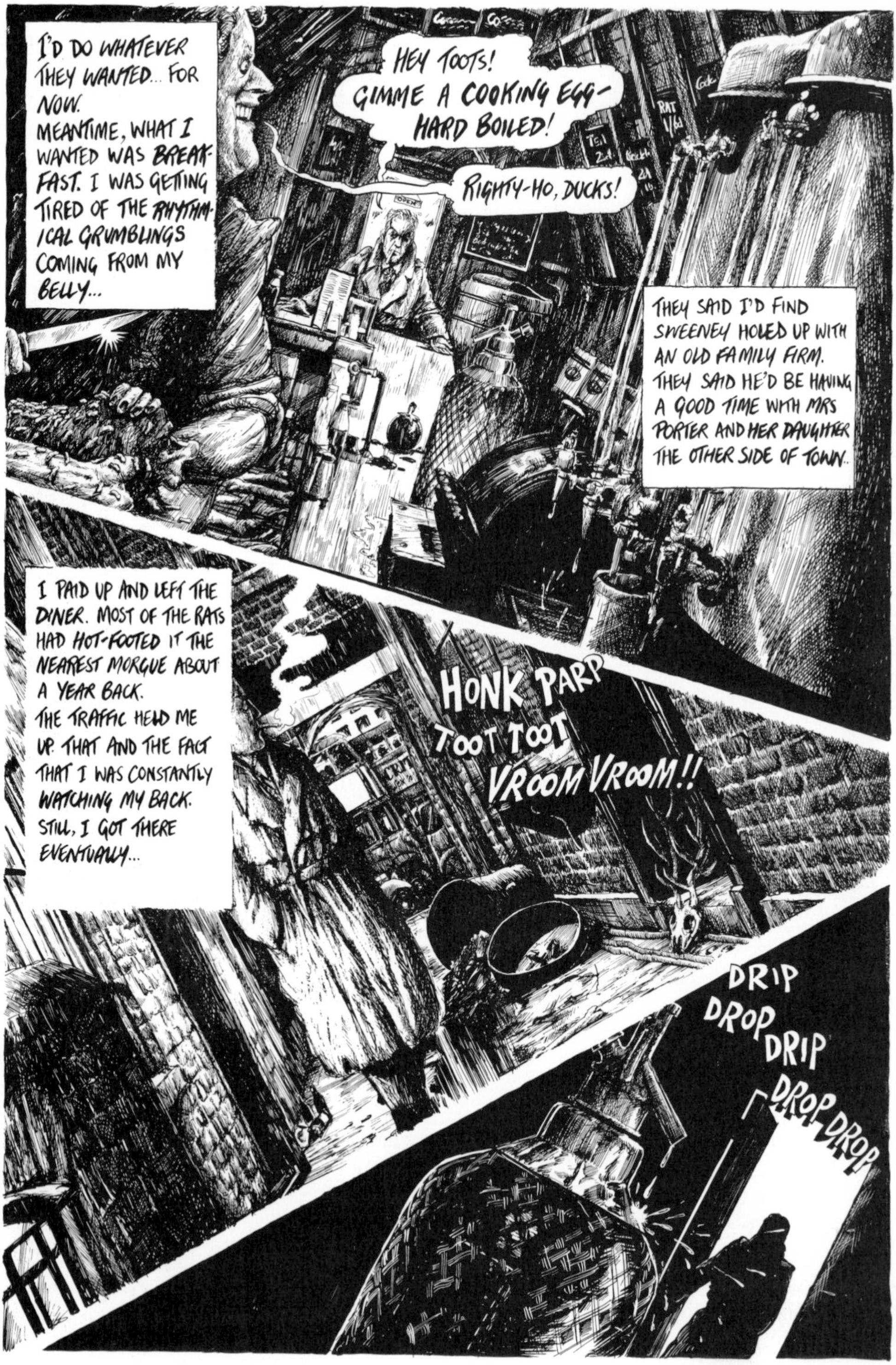
I'D DO WHATEVER THEY WANTED... FOR NOW.
MEANTIME, WHAT I WANTED WAS BREAKFAST. I WAS GETTING TIRED OF THE RHYTHMICAL GRUMBLINGS COMING FROM MY BELLY...
HEY TOOTS! GIMME A COOKING EGG - HARD BOILED!
RIGHTY-HO, DUCKS!
THEY SAID I'D FIND SWEENEY HOLED UP WITH AN OLD FAMILY FIRM.
THEY SAID HE'D BE HAVING A GOOD TIME WITH MRS PORTER AND HER DAUGHTER THE OTHER SIDE OF TOWN...
I PAID UP AND LEFT THE DINER. MOST OF THE RATS HAD HOT-FOOTED IT THE NEAREST MORGUE ABOUT A YEAR BACK.
THE TRAFFIC HELD ME UP. THAT AND THE FACT THAT I WAS CONSTANTLY WATCHING MY BACK.
STILL, I GOT THERE EVENTUALLY...
HONK PARP
TOOT TOOT
VROOM VROOM!!
DRIP
DROP DRIP
DROP DROP

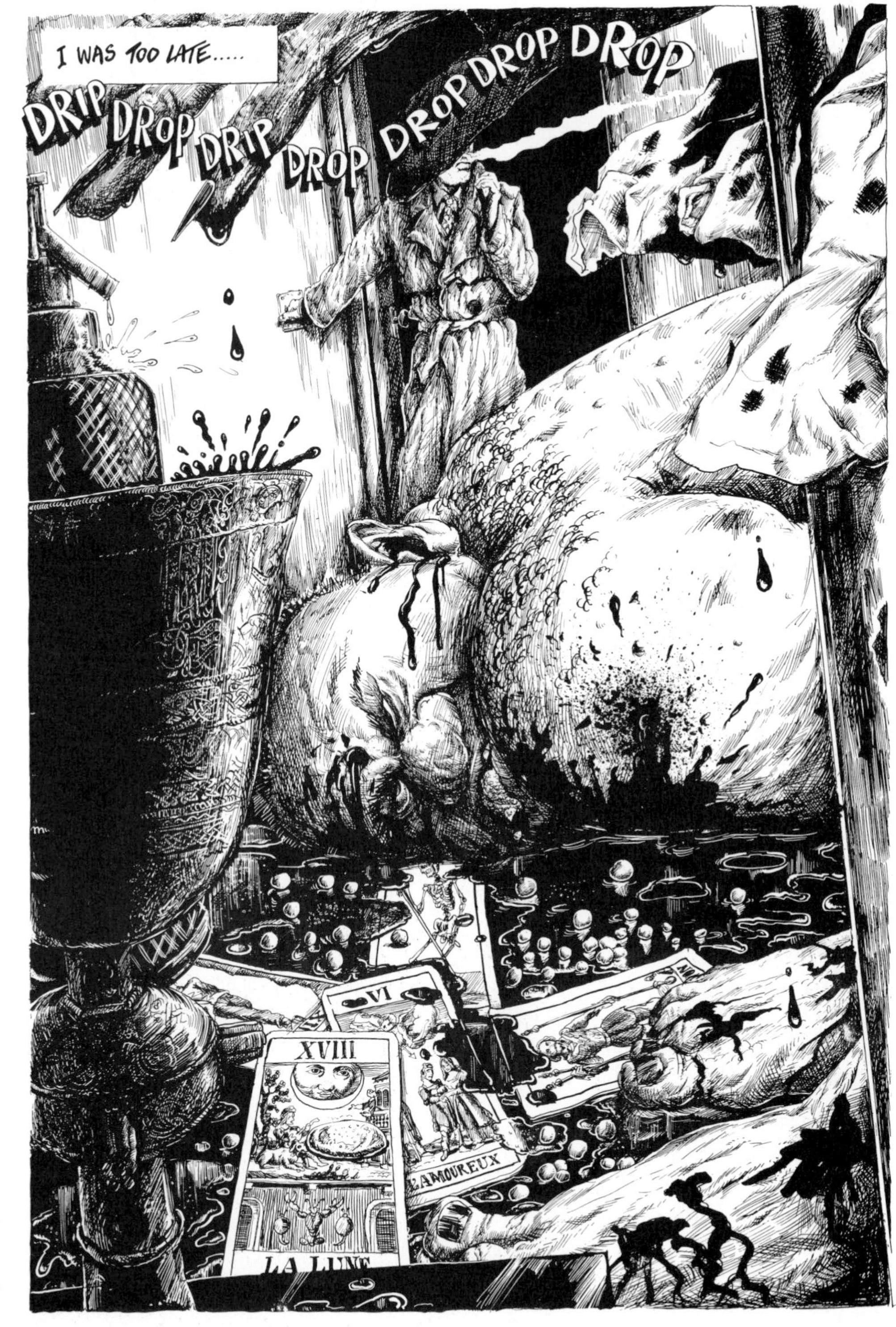
I WAS TOO LATE.....
DRIP DROP DRIP DROP DROP DROP DROP
XVIII
LA LUNE
VI
L'AMOUREUX

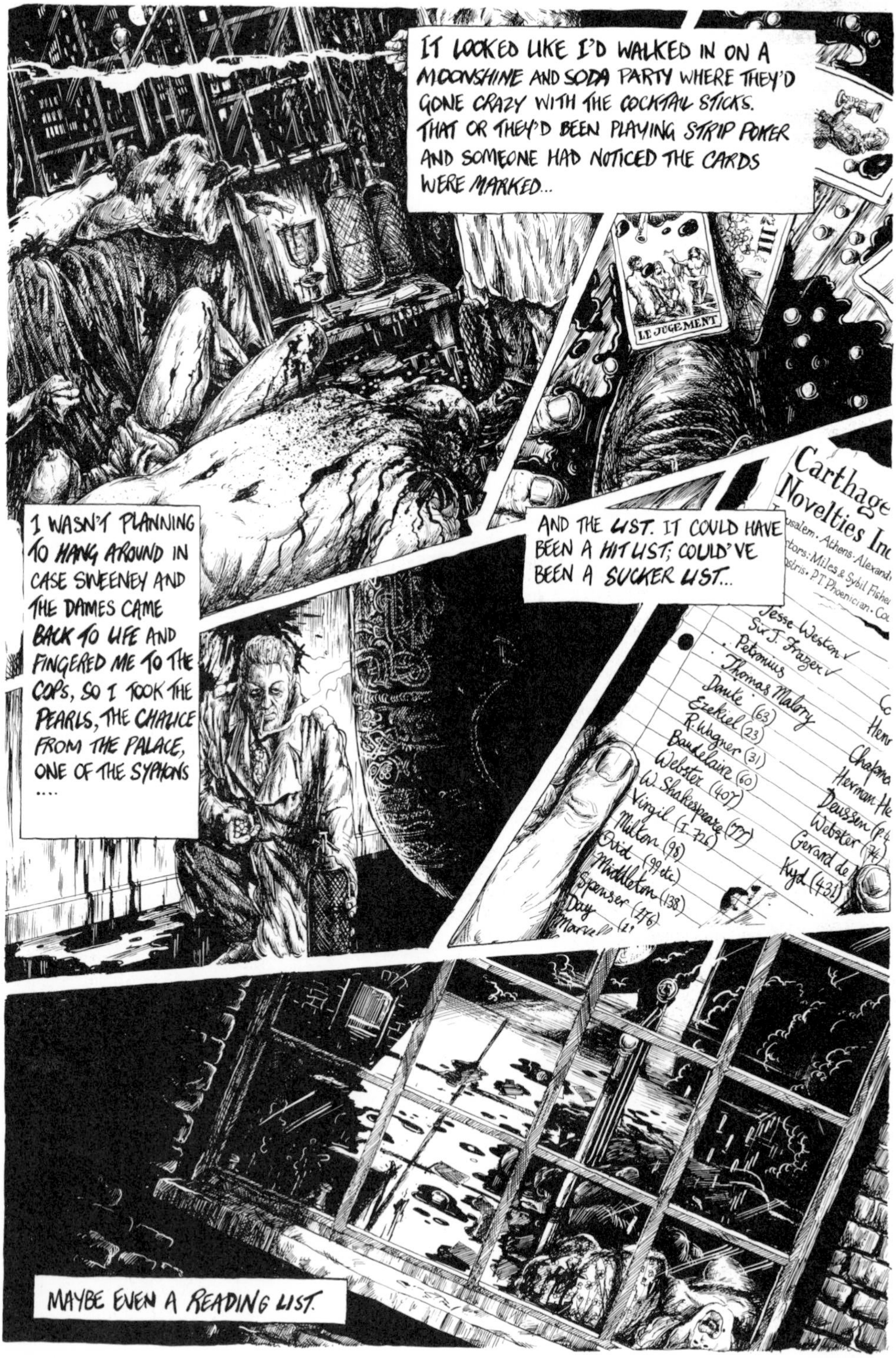
IT LOOKED LIKE I'D WALKED IN ON A MOONSHINE AND SODA PARTY WHERE THEY'D GONE CRAZY WITH THE COCKTAIL STICKS. THAT OR THEY'D BEEN PLAYING STRIP POKER AND SOMEONE HAD NOTICED THE CARDS WERE MARKED...
LE JUGEMENT
I WASN'T PLANNING TO HANG AROUND IN CASE SWEENEY AND THE DAMES CAME BACK TO LIFE AND FINGERED ME TO THE COPS, SO I TOOK THE PEARLS, THE CHALICE FROM THE PALACE, ONE OF THE SYPHONS ....
AND THE LIST. IT COULD HAVE BEEN A HIT LIST; COULD'VE BEEN A SUCKER LIST...
Carthage
Jesse Weston ✓
Sir J. Frazer ✓
Petronius
Thomas Malory
Dante (63)
Ezekiel (23)
R. Wagner (31)
Baudelaire (60)
Webster (407)
W. Shakespeare (77)
Virgil (I. 726)
Milton (98)
Ovid (99 etc)
Middleton (138)
Spenser (276)
Day
Kyd (431)
MAYBE EVEN A READING LIST.

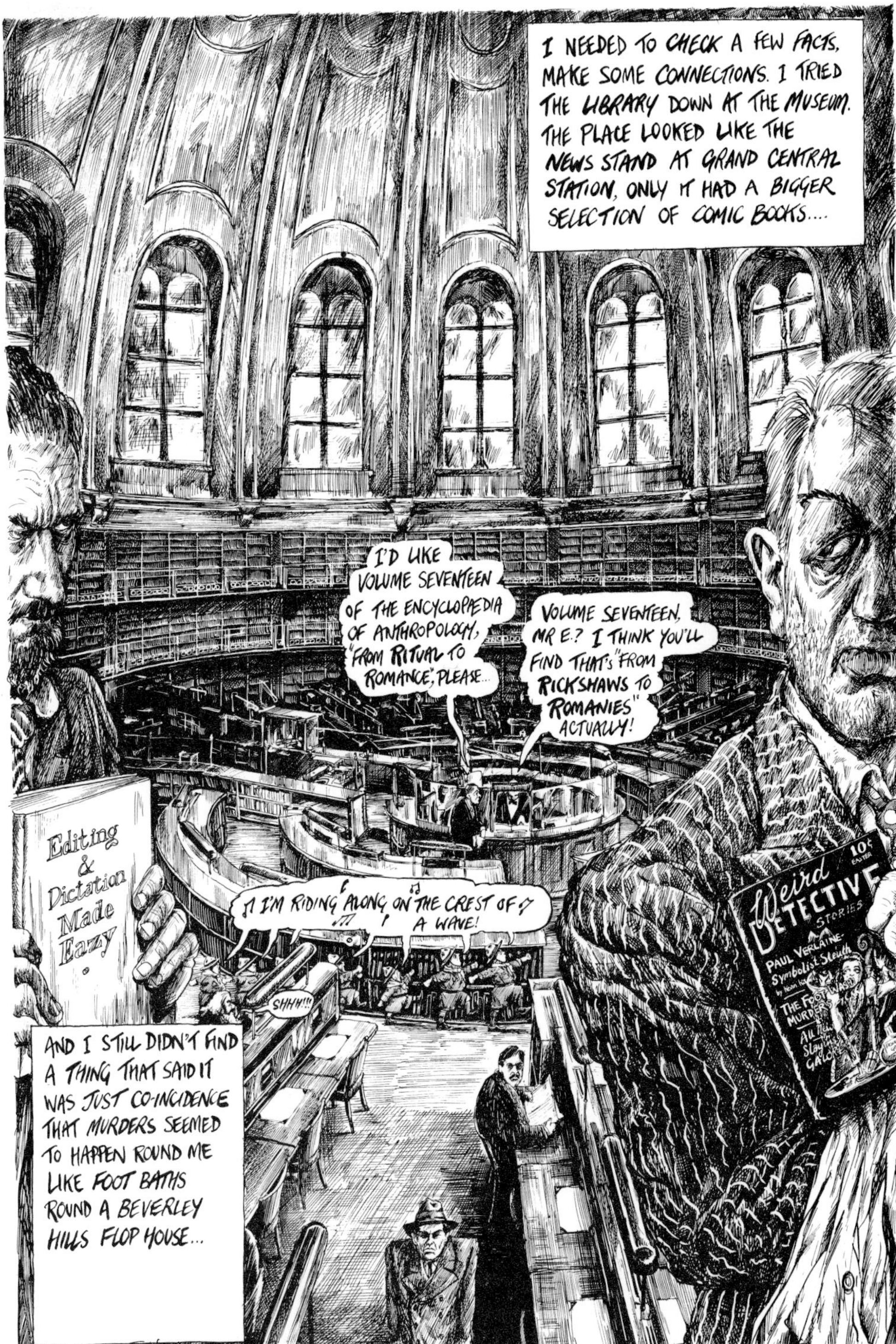

I NEEDED TO CHECK A FEW FACTS, MAKE SOME CONNECTIONS. I TRIED THE LIBRARY DOWN AT THE MUSEUM. THE PLACE LOOKED LIKE THE NEWS STAND AT GRAND CENTRAL STATION, ONLY IT HAD A BIGGER SELECTION OF COMIC BOOKS....
I'D LIKE VOLUME SEVENTEEN OF THE ENCYCLOPAEDIA OF ANTHROPOLOGY, "FROM RITUAL TO ROMANCE", PLEASE...
VOLUME SEVENTEEN, MR E.? I THINK YOU'LL FIND THAT'S "FROM RICKSHAWS TO ROMANIES" ACTUALLY!
Editing & Dictation Made Eazy
I'M RIDING ALONG ON THE CREST OF A WAVE!
SHHH!!!
Weird DETECTIVE STORIES
10¢
PAUL VERLAINE - Symbolist Sleuth
THE FOOT WASH MURDERS
AND I STILL DIDN'T FIND A THING THAT SAID IT WAS JUST CO-INCIDENCE THAT MURDERS SEEMED TO HAPPEN ROUND ME LIKE FOOT BATHS ROUND A BEVERLEY HILLS FLOP HOUSE...

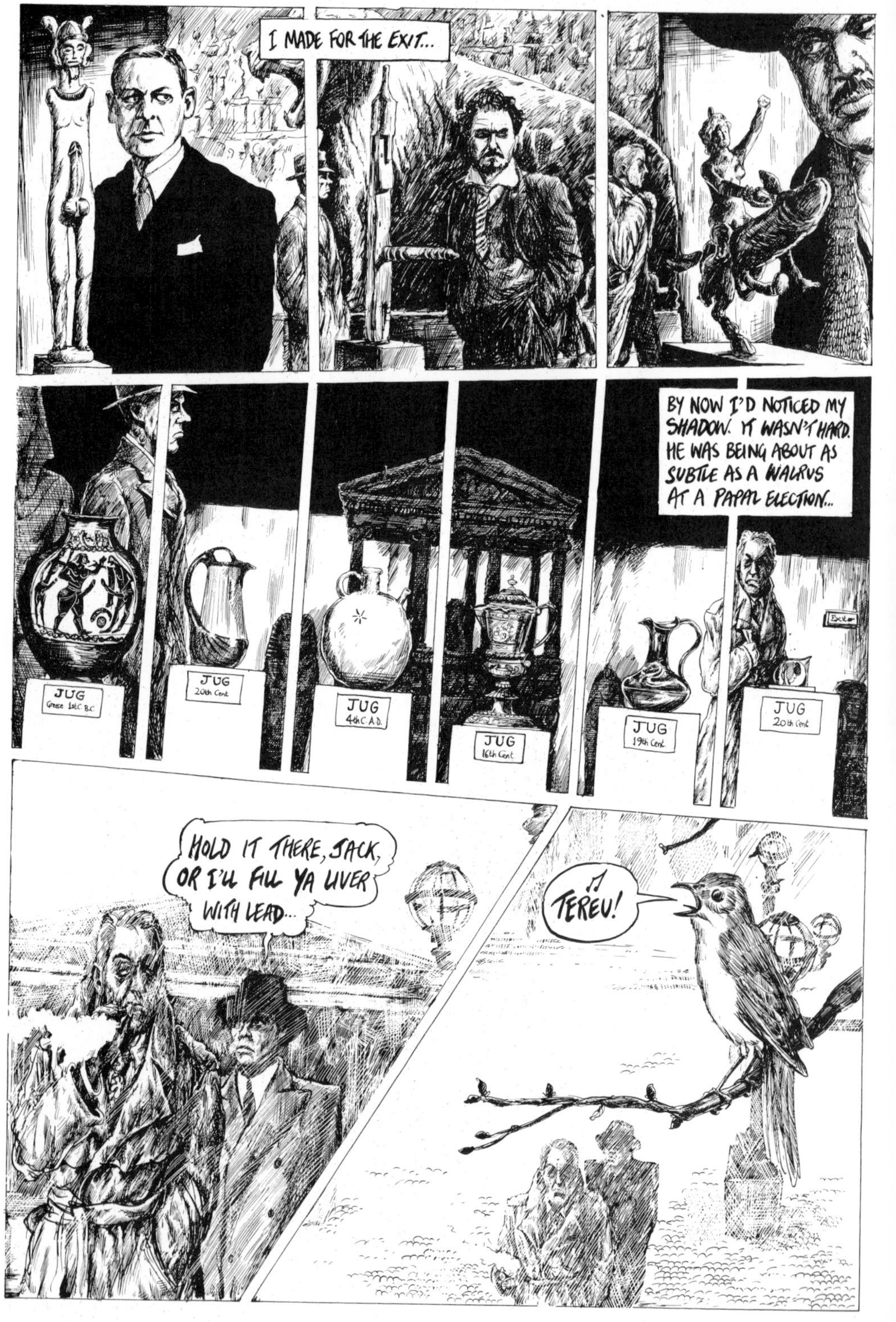
I MADE FOR THE EXIT...
BY NOW I'D NOTICED MY SHADOW. IT WASN'T HARD. HE WAS BEING ABOUT AS SUBTLE AS A WALRUS AT A PAPAL ELECTION...
JUG
Grece 1stC. B.C.
JUG
20th Cent
JUG
4th C. A.D.
JUG
16th Cent
JUG
19th Cent
JUG
20th Cent
Exit
HOLD IT THERE, JACK, OR I'LL FILL YA LIVER WITH LEAD...
TEREU!

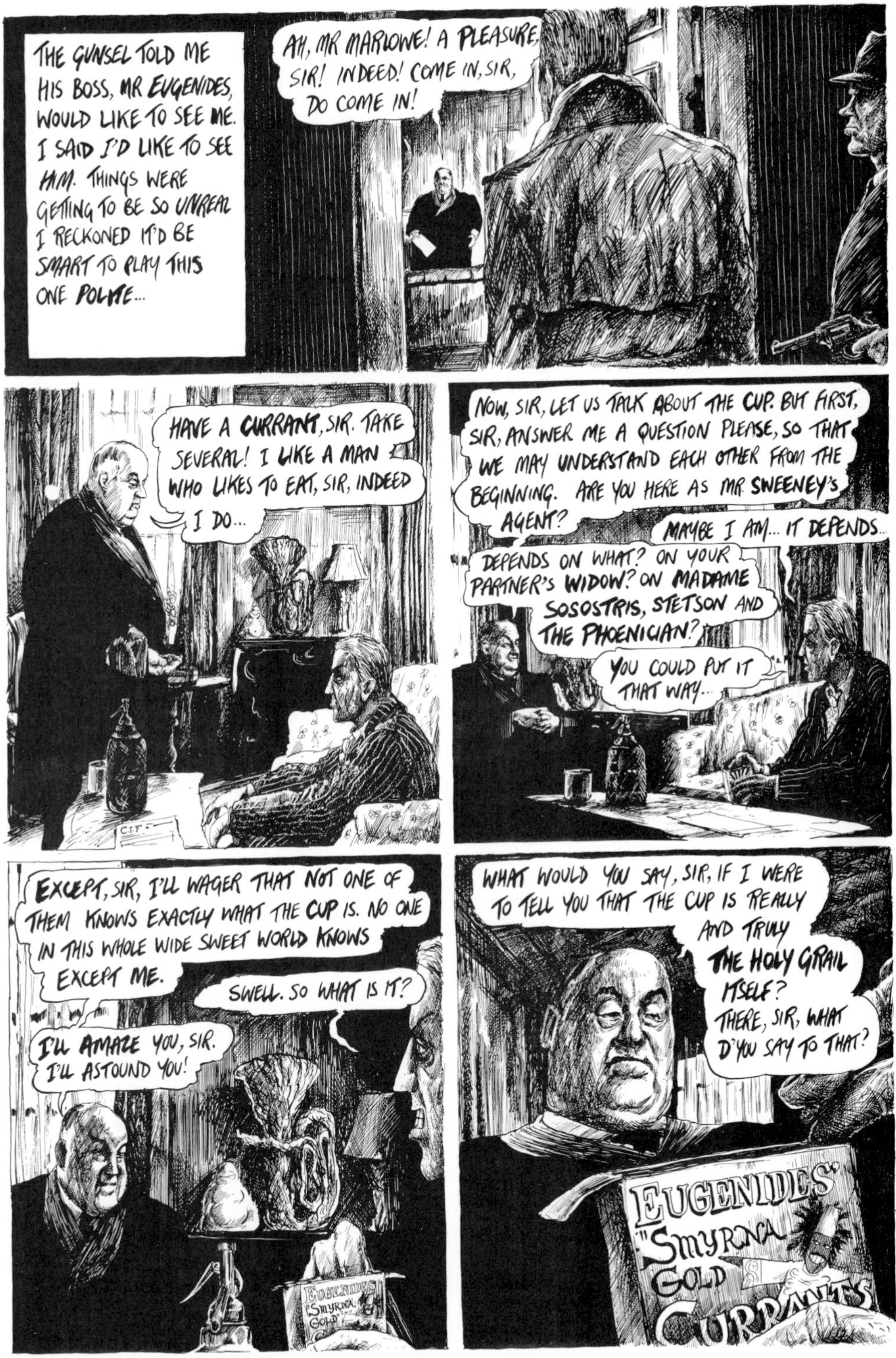
THE GUNSEL TOLD ME HIS BOSS, MR EUGENIDES, WOULD LIKE TO SEE ME. I SAID I'D LIKE TO SEE HIM. THINGS WERE GETTING TO BE SO UNREAL I RECKONED IT'D BE SMART TO PLAY THIS ONE POLITE...
AH, MR MARLOWE! A PLEASURE, SIR! INDEED! COME IN, SIR, DO COME IN!
HAVE A CURRANT, SIR. TAKE SEVERAL! I LIKE A MAN WHO LIKES TO EAT, SIR, INDEED I DO...
C.I.F.
NOW, SIR, LET US TALK ABOUT THE CUP. BUT FIRST, SIR, ANSWER ME A QUESTION PLEASE, SO THAT WE MAY UNDERSTAND EACH OTHER FROM THE BEGINNING. ARE YOU HERE AS MR SWEENEY'S AGENT?
MAYBE I AM... IT DEPENDS...
DEPENDS ON WHAT? ON YOUR PARTNER'S WIDOW? ON MADAME SOSOSTRIS, STETSON AND THE PHOENICIAN?
YOU COULD PUT IT THAT WAY...
EXCEPT, SIR, I'LL WAGER THAT NOT ONE OF THEM KNOWS EXACTLY WHAT THE CUP IS. NO ONE IN THIS WHOLE WIDE SWEET WORLD KNOWS EXCEPT ME.
SWELL. SO WHAT IS IT?
I'LL AMAZE YOU, SIR. I'LL ASTOUND YOU!
EUGENIDES' "SMYRNA GOLD
WHAT WOULD YOU SAY, SIR, IF I WERE TO TELL YOU THAT THE CUP IS REALLY AND TRULY THE HOLY GRAIL ITSELF? THERE, SIR, WHAT D'YOU SAY TO THAT?
EUGENIDES' "SMYRNA GOLD CURRANTS

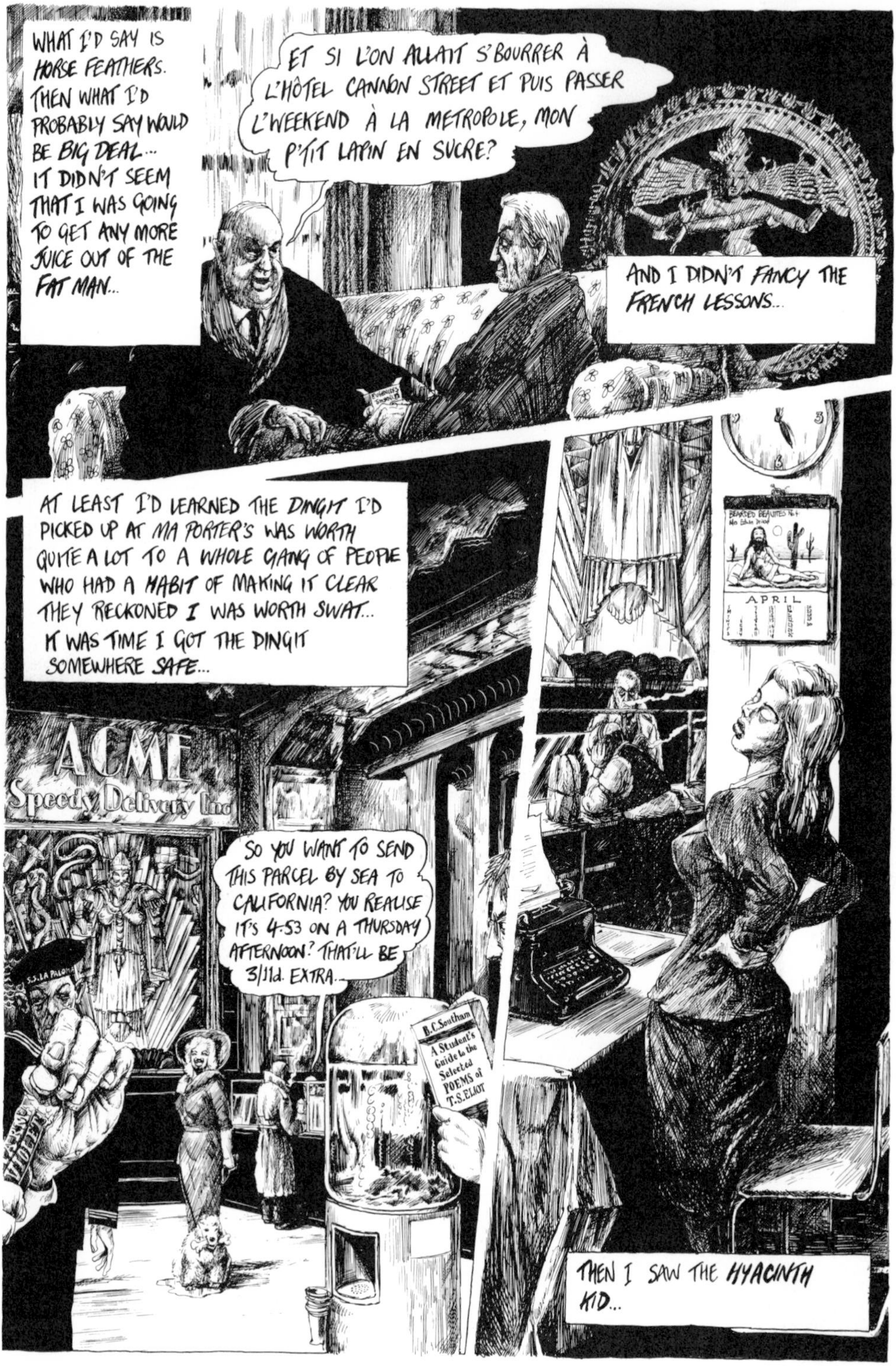
WHAT I'D SAY IS HORSE FEATHERS. THEN WHAT I'D PROBABLY SAY WOULD BE BIG DEAL... IT DIDN'T SEEM THAT I WAS GOING TO GET ANY MORE JUICE OUT OF THE FAT MAN...
ET SI L'ON ALLAIT S'BOURRER À L'HÔTEL CANNON STREET ET PUIS PASSER L'WEEKEND À LA METROPOLE, MON P'TIT LAPIN EN SUCRE?
AND I DIDN'T FANCY THE FRENCH LESSONS...
AT LEAST I'D LEARNED THE DINGIT I'D PICKED UP AT MA PORTER'S WAS WORTH QUITE A LOT TO A WHOLE GANG OF PEOPLE WHO HAD A HABIT OF MAKING IT CLEAR THEY RECKONED I WAS WORTH SWAT... IT WAS TIME I GOT THE DINGIT SOMEWHERE SAFE...
ACME
Speedy Delivery Inc
APRIL
SO YOU WANT TO SEND THIS PARCEL BY SEA TO CALIFORNIA? YOU REALISE IT'S 4:53 ON A THURSDAY AFTERNOON? THAT'LL BE 3/11d. EXTRA...
B.C.Southam
A Student's Guide to the Selected POEMS of T.S.ELIOT
THEN I SAW THE HYACINTH KID...

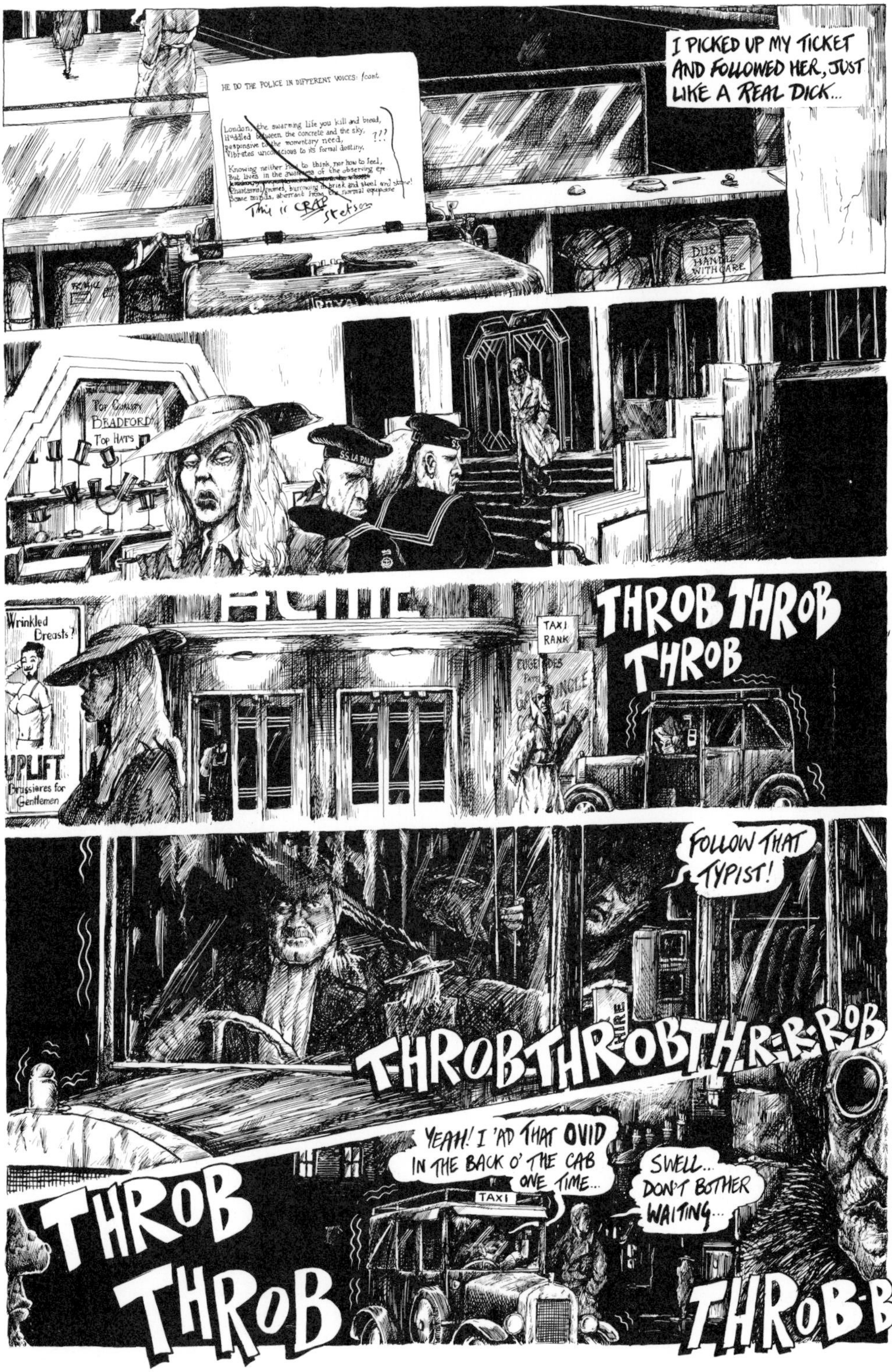
HE DO THE POLICE IN DIFFERENT VOICES: /cont.
London, the swarming life you kill and breed,
Huddled between the concrete and the sky,
Responsive to the momentary need,
Vibrates unconscious to its formal destiny,
Knowing neither how to think, nor how to feel,
But lives in the awareness of the observing eye.
Phantasmal gnomes, burrowing in brick and steel and stone!
Some minds, aberrant from the normal equipoise
???
This is CRAP
Stetson
I PICKED UP MY TICKET AND FOLLOWED HER, JUST LIKE A REAL DICK...
DUST
HANDLE WITH CARE
ROYAL
Top Quality
BRADFORD
Top Hats
SS LA PALL
Wrinkled Breasts?
UPLIFT
Brassieres for Gentlemen
TAXI RANK
THROB THROB THROB
FOLLOW THAT TYPIST!
HIRE
T-H-R-O-B-THROB-T-H-R-R-R-ROB
YEAH! I 'AD THAT OVID IN THE BACK O' THE CAB ONE TIME...
SWELL... DON'T BOTHER WAITING...
TAXI
THROB THROB
THROB-B-

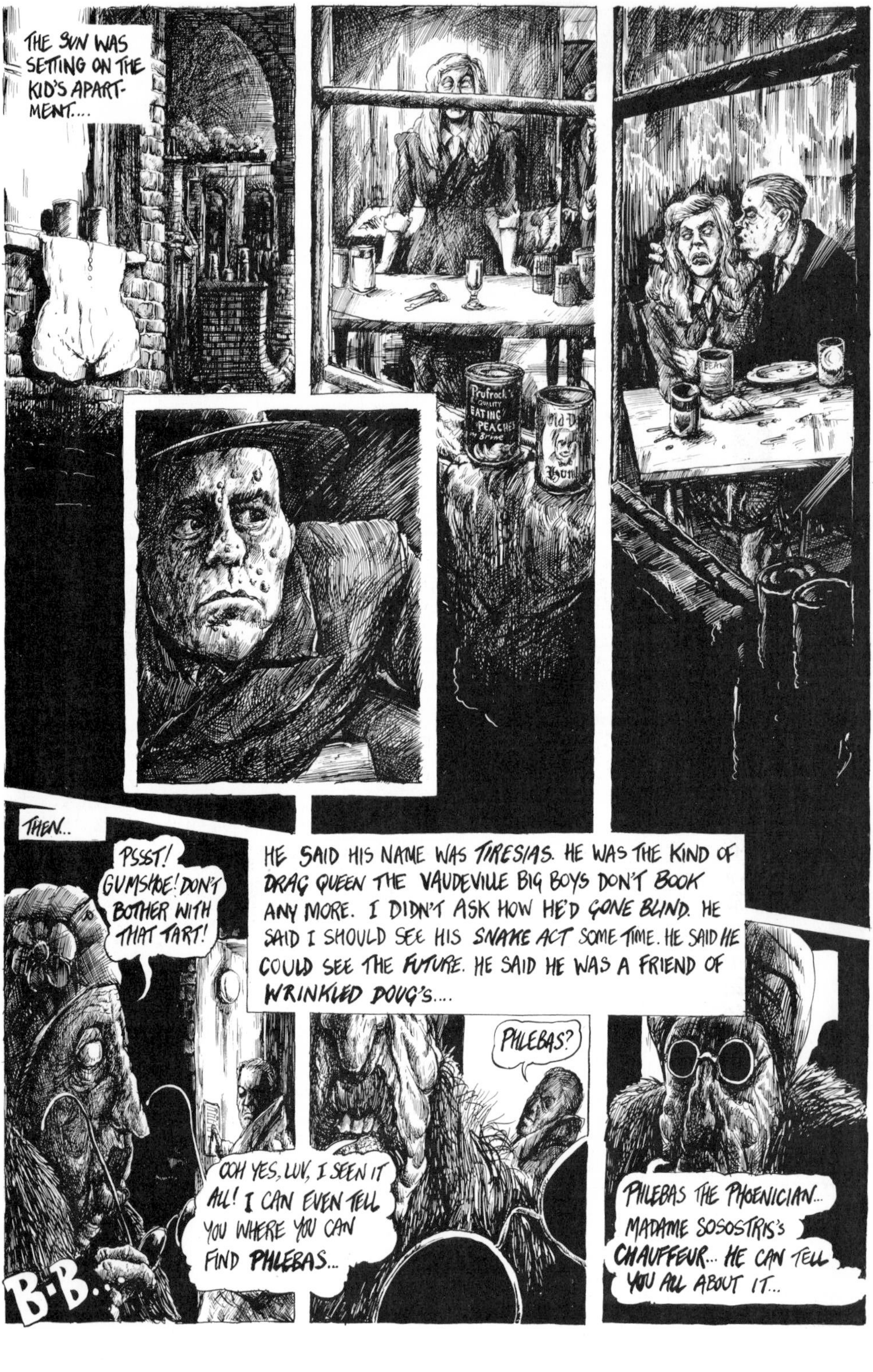
THE SUN WAS SETTING ON THE KID'S APARTMENT....
Prufrock's QUALITY EATING PEACHES in Brine
THEN...
PSSST! GUMSHOE! DON'T BOTHER WITH THAT TART!
HE SAID HIS NAME WAS TIRESIAS. HE WAS THE KIND OF DRAG QUEEN THE VAUDEVILLE BIG BOYS DON'T BOOK ANY MORE. I DIDN'T ASK HOW HE'D GONE BLIND. HE SAID I SHOULD SEE HIS SNAKE ACT SOME TIME. HE SAID HE COULD SEE THE FUTURE. HE SAID HE WAS A FRIEND OF WRINKLED DOUG'S....
B-B...
OOH YES, LUV, I SEEN IT ALL! I CAN EVEN TELL YOU WHERE YOU CAN FIND PHLEBAS...
PHLEBAS?
PHLEBAS THE PHOENICIAN... MADAME SOSOSTRIS'S CHAUFFEUR... HE CAN TELL YOU ALL ABOUT IT...

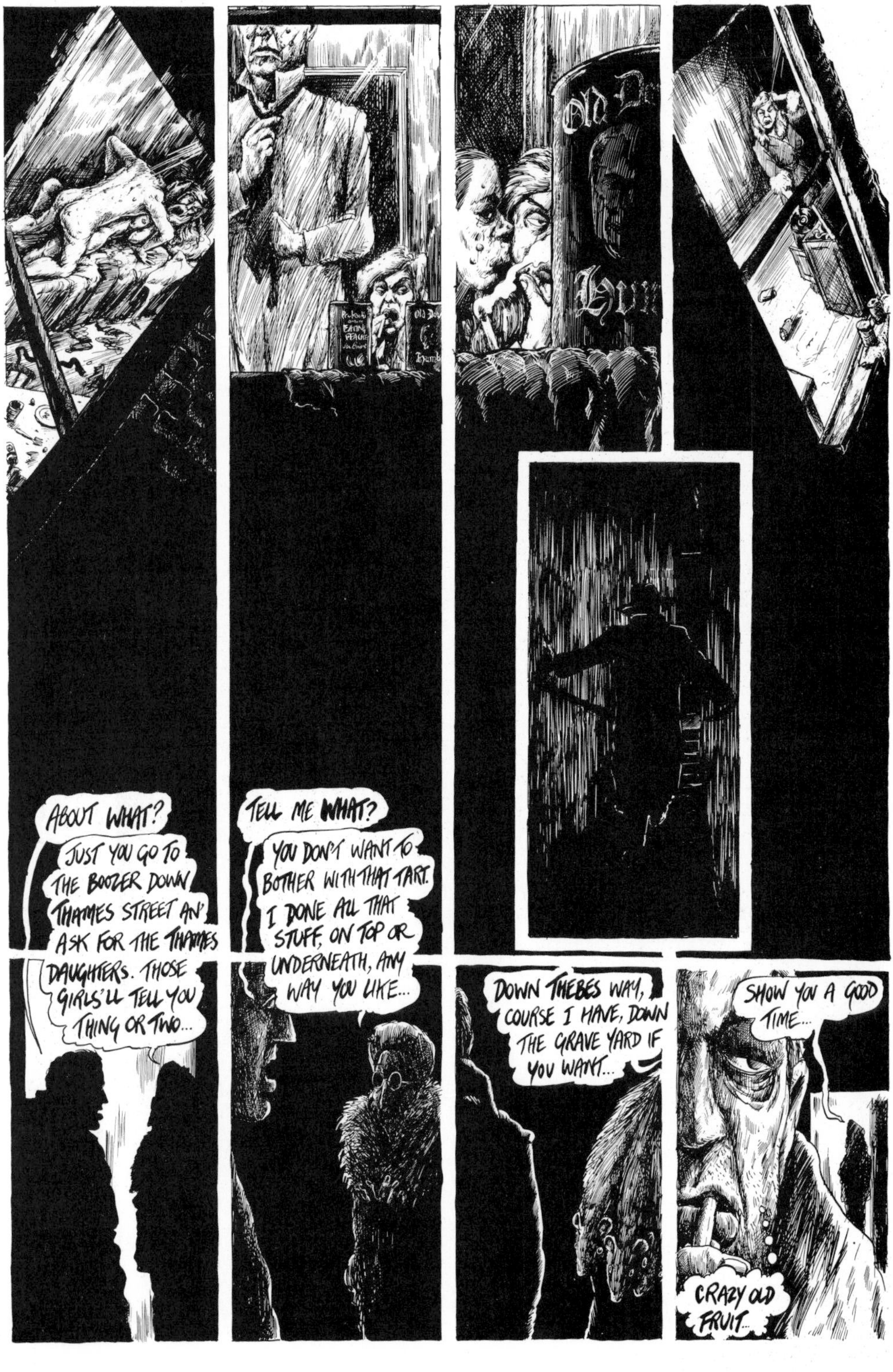
ABOUT WHAT?
JUST YOU GO TO THE BOOZER DOWN THAMES STREET AN' ASK FOR THE THAMES DAUGHTERS. THOSE GIRLS'LL TELL YOU THING OR TWO...
TELL ME WHAT?
YOU DON'T WANT TO BOTHER WITH THAT TART. I DONE ALL THAT STUFF, ON TOP OR UNDERNEATH, ANY WAY YOU LIKE...
DOWN THEBES WAY, COURSE I HAVE, DOWN THE GRAVE YARD IF YOU WANT...
SHOW YOU A GOOD TIME...
CRAZY OLD FRUIT...

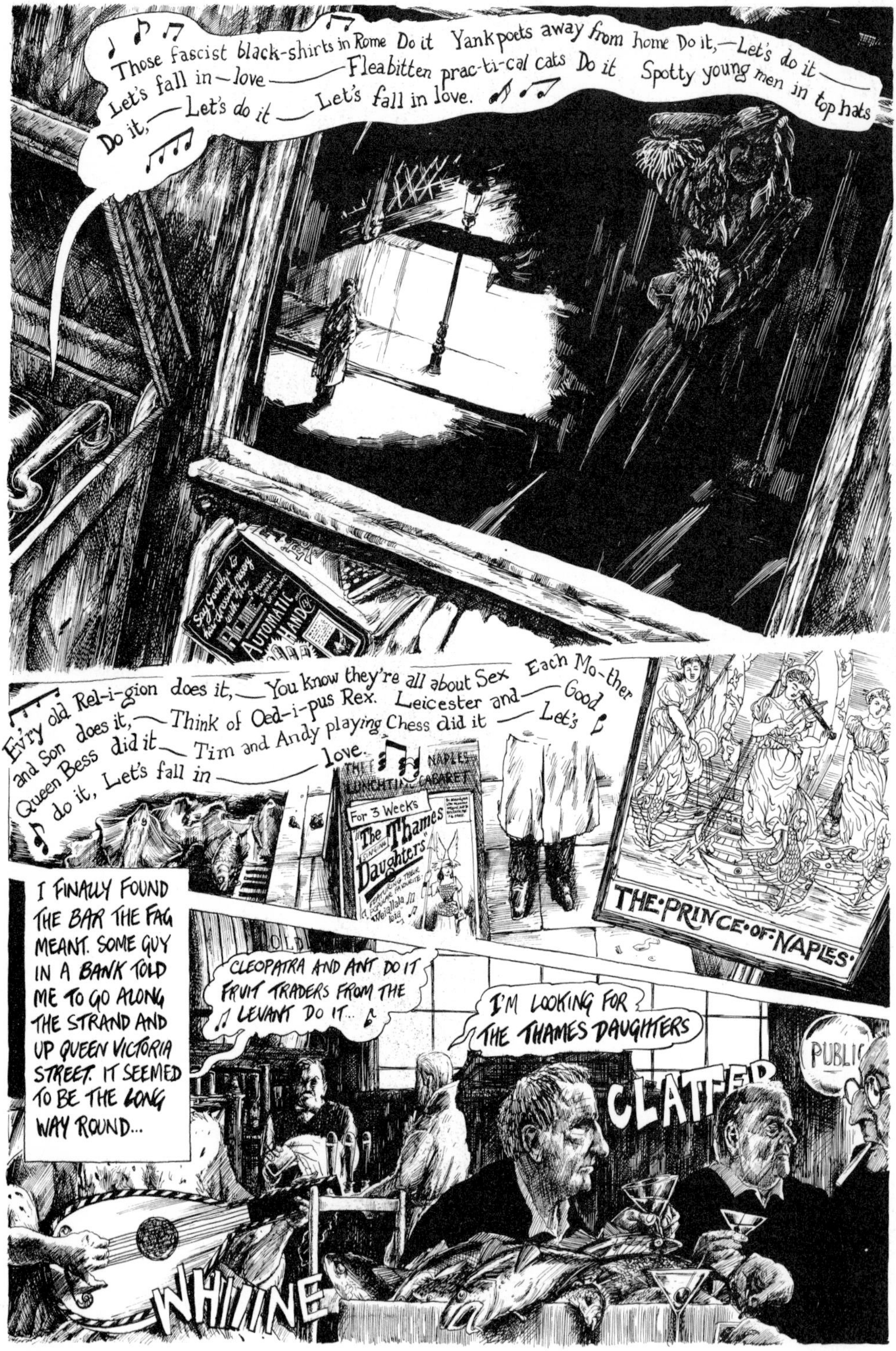
Those fascist black-shirts in Rome Do it Yank poets away from home Do it, —Let's do it — Let's fall in — love — Fleabitten prac-ti-cal cats Do it Spotty young men in top hats Do it, — Let's do it — Let's fall in love.
Say Goodbye to hair dressing misery with the
MONEY SAVING UP-TO-DATE
AUTOMATIC HAND
Ev'ry old Rel-i-gion does it, — You know they're all about Sex Each Mo-ther and Son does it, — Think of Oed-i-pus Rex. Leicester and — Good Queen Bess did it — Tim and Andy playing Chess did it — Let's do it, Let's fall in — love.
LUNCHTIME CABARET
For 3 Weeks
"The Singing Thames Daughters"
FEATURING THEIR POPULAR FAVOURITE: "Weiallala leia"
THE·PRINCE·OF·NAPLES·
I FINALLY FOUND THE BAR THE FAG MEANT. SOME GUY IN A BANK TOLD ME TO GO ALONG THE STRAND AND UP QUEEN VICTORIA STREET. IT SEEMED TO BE THE LONG WAY ROUND...
CLEOPATRA AND ANT DO IT FRUIT TRADERS FROM THE LEVANT DO IT...
I'M LOOKING FOR THE THAMES DAUGHTERS
PUBLIC
CLATTER
WHIIINE

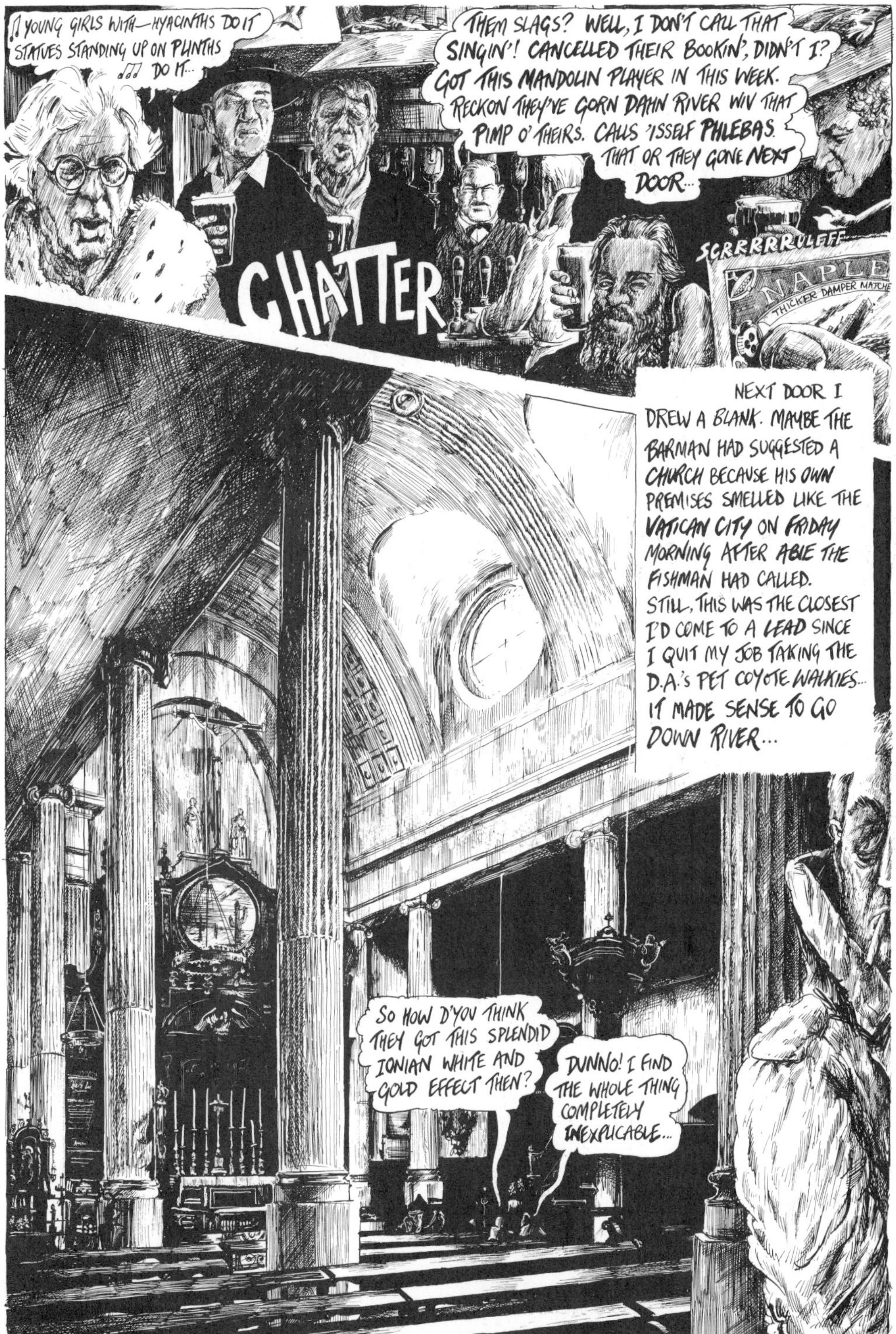
YOUNG GIRLS WITH—HYACINTHS DO IT STATUES STANDING UP ON PLINTHS DO IT...
THEM SLAGS? WELL, I DON'T CALL THAT SINGIN'! CANCELLED THEIR BOOKIN', DIDN'T I? GOT THIS MANDOLIN PLAYER IN THIS WEEK. RECKON THEY'VE GORN DAHN RIVER WIV THAT PIMP O' THEIRS. CALLS 'ISSELF PHLEBAS. THAT OR THEY GONE NEXT DOOR...
CHATTER
SCRRRRRULEFF
NEXT DOOR I DREW A BLANK. MAYBE THE BARMAN HAD SUGGESTED A CHURCH BECAUSE HIS OWN PREMISES SMELLED LIKE THE VATICAN CITY ON FRIDAY MORNING AFTER ABIE THE FISHMAN HAD CALLED. STILL, THIS WAS THE CLOSEST I'D COME TO A LEAD SINCE I QUIT MY JOB TAKING THE D.A.'S PET COYOTE WALKIES... IT MADE SENSE TO GO DOWN RIVER...
SO HOW D'YOU THINK THEY GOT THIS SPLENDID IONIAN WHITE AND GOLD EFFECT THEN?
DUNNO! I FIND THE WHOLE THING COMPLETELY INEXPLICABLE...

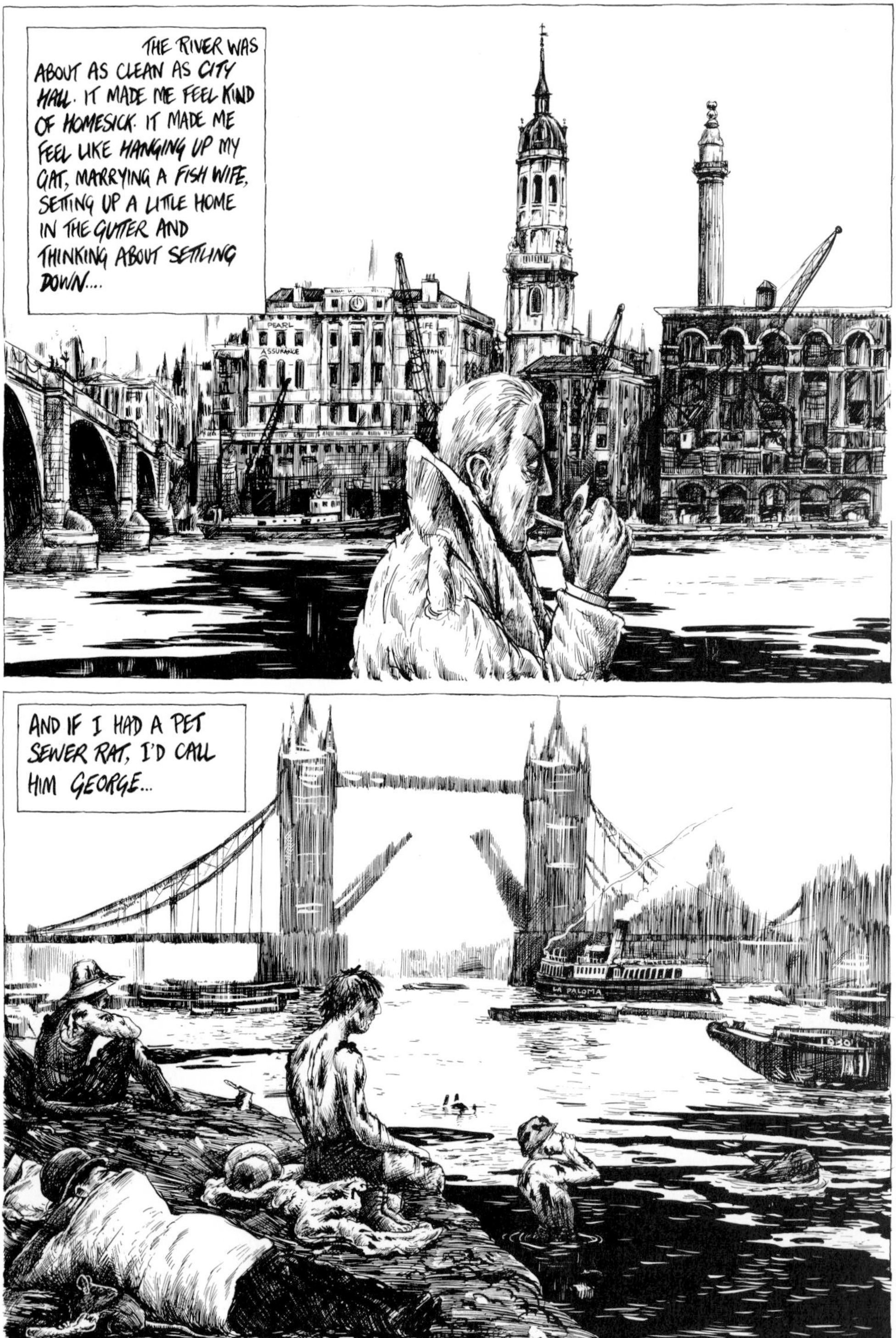
THE RIVER WAS ABOUT AS CLEAN AS CITY HALL. IT MADE ME FEEL KIND OF HOMESICK. IT MADE ME FEEL LIKE HANGING UP MY GAT, MARRYING A FISH WIFE, SETTING UP A LITTLE HOME IN THE GUTTER AND THINKING ABOUT SETTLING DOWN....
AND IF I HAD A PET SEWER RAT, I'D CALL HIM GEORGE...

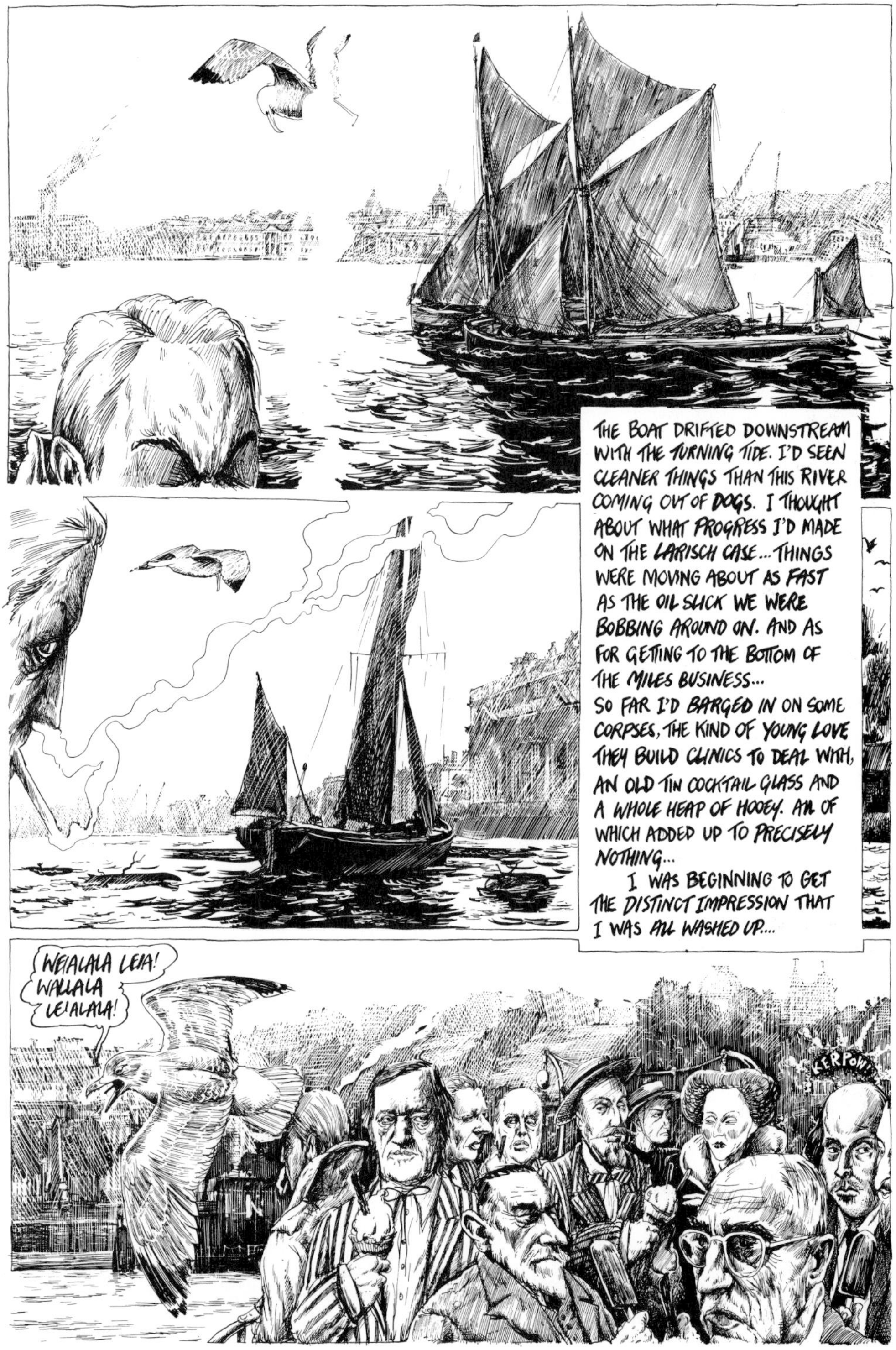
THE BOAT DRIFTED DOWNSTREAM WITH THE TURNING TIDE. I'D SEEN CLEANER THINGS THAN THIS RIVER COMING OUT OF DOGS. I THOUGHT ABOUT WHAT PROGRESS I'D MADE ON THE LARISCH CASE... THINGS WERE MOVING ABOUT AS FAST AS THE OIL SLICK WE WERE BOBBING AROUND ON. AND AS FOR GETTING TO THE BOTTOM OF THE MILES BUSINESS...
SO FAR I'D BARGED IN ON SOME CORPSES, THE KIND OF YOUNG LOVE THEY BUILD CLINICS TO DEAL WITH, AN OLD TIN COCKTAIL GLASS AND A WHOLE HEAP OF HOOEY. ALL OF WHICH ADDED UP TO PRECISELY NOTHING...
I WAS BEGINNING TO GET THE DISTINCT IMPRESSION THAT I WAS ALL WASHED UP....
WEIALALA LEIA! WALLALA LEIALALA!
KERPOW!

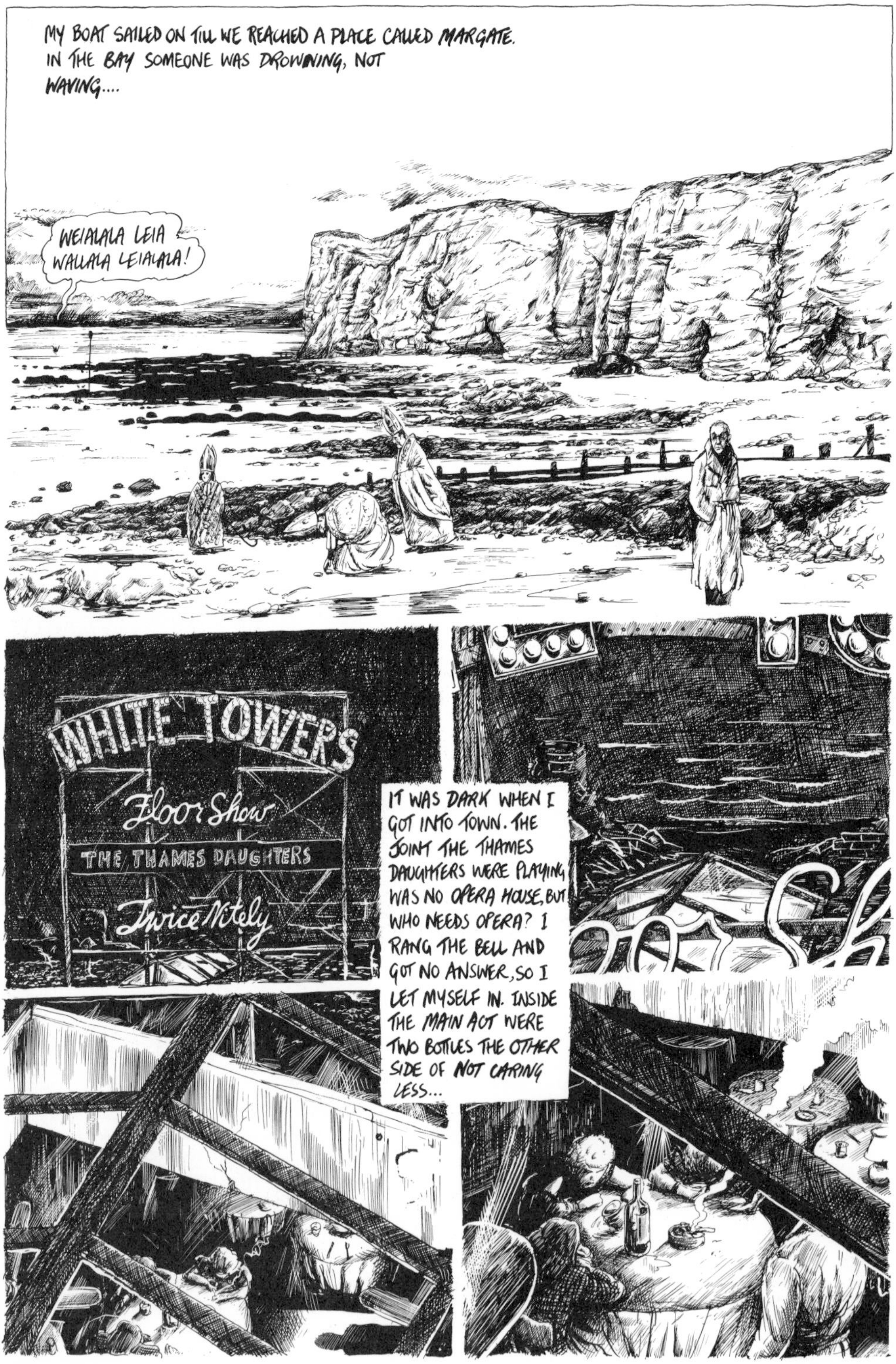
MY BOAT SAILED ON TILL WE REACHED A PLACE CALLED MARGATE. IN THE BAY SOMEONE WAS DROWNING, NOT WAVING....
WEIALALA LEIA WALLALA LEIALALA!
WHITE TOWERS
Floor Show
THE THAMES DAUGHTERS
Twice Nitely
IT WAS DARK WHEN I GOT INTO TOWN. THE JOINT THE THAMES DAUGHTERS WERE PLAYING WAS NO OPERA HOUSE, BUT WHO NEEDS OPERA? I RANG THE BELL AND GOT NO ANSWER, SO I LET MYSELF IN. INSIDE THE MAIN ACT WERE TWO BOTTLES THE OTHER SIDE OF NOT CARING LESS...

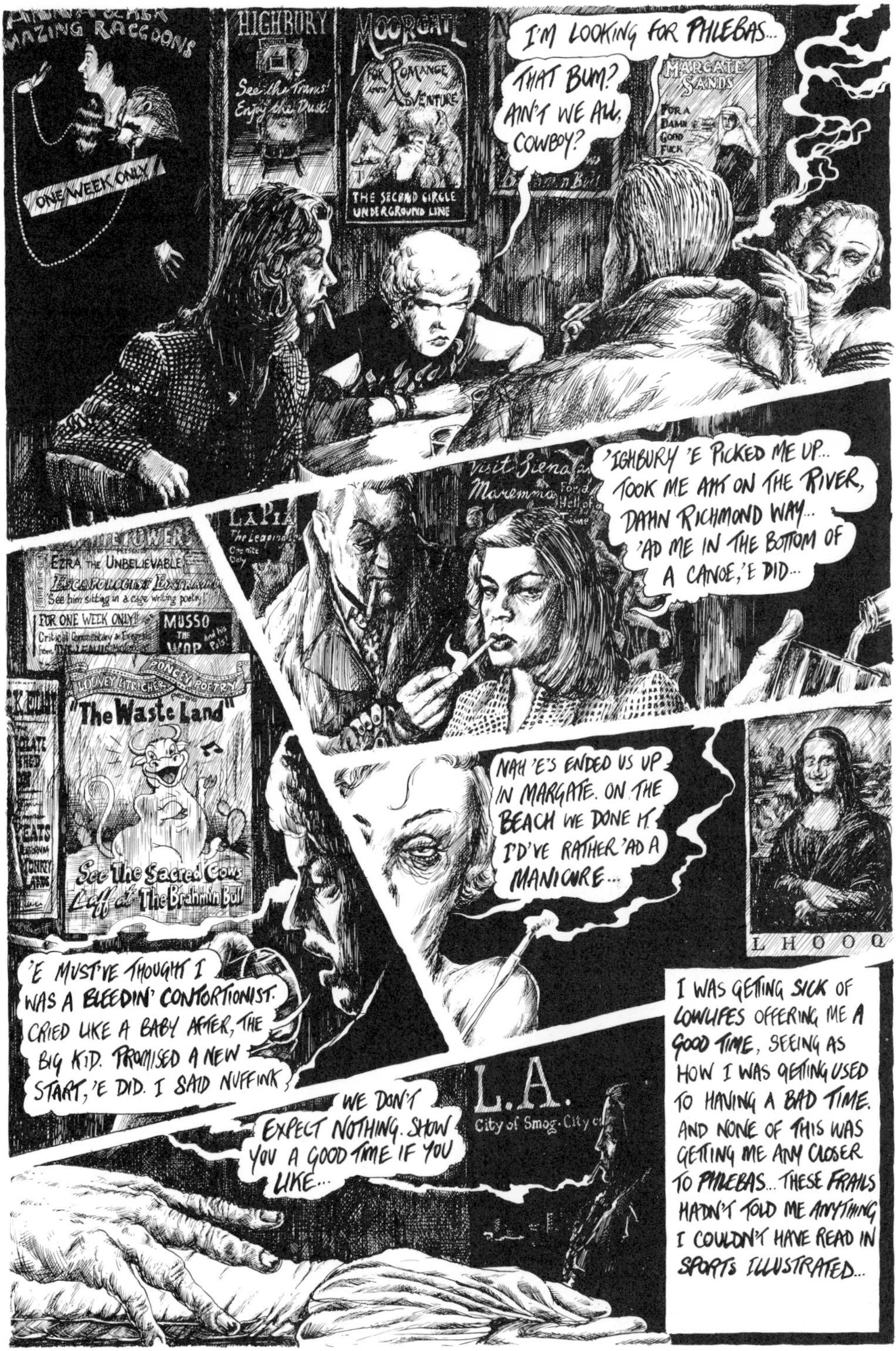
HIGHBURY
See the Trams! Enjoy the Dust!
MOORGATE
FOR ROMANCE AND ADVENTURE
THE SECOND CIRCLE UNDERGROUND LINE
MARGATE SANDS
FOR A DAMN GOOD FUCK
ONE WEEK ONLY
I'M LOOKING FOR PHLEBAS...
THAT BUM? AIN'T WE ALL, COWBOY?
'IGHBURY 'E PICKED ME UP... TOOK ME AHT ON THE RIVER, DAHN RICHMOND WAY... 'AD ME IN THE BOTTOM OF A CANOE, 'E DID...
EZRA THE UNBELIEVABLE
See him sitting in a cage writing poetry!
FOR ONE WEEK ONLY!!
MUSSO THE WOP
LOONEY LITRICHER
PONCEY POETRY
"The Waste Land"
See The Sacred Cows Laff at The Brahmin Bull
NAH 'E'S ENDED US UP IN MARGATE. ON THE BEACH WE DONE IT. I'D'VE RATHER 'AD A MANICURE...
LHOOQ
'E MUST'VE THOUGHT I WAS A BLEEDIN' CONTORTIONIST. CRIED LIKE A BABY AFTER, THE BIG KID. PROMISED A NEW START, 'E DID. I SAID NUFFINK.
WE DON'T EXPECT NOTHING. SHOW YOU A GOOD TIME IF YOU LIKE...
L.A.
I WAS GETTING SICK OF LOWLIFES OFFERING ME A GOOD TIME, SEEING AS HOW I WAS GETTING USED TO HAVING A BAD TIME. AND NONE OF THIS WAS GETTING ME ANY CLOSER TO PHLEBAS... THESE FRAILS HADN'T TOLD ME ANYTHING I COULDN'T HAVE READ IN SPORTS ILLUSTRATED...

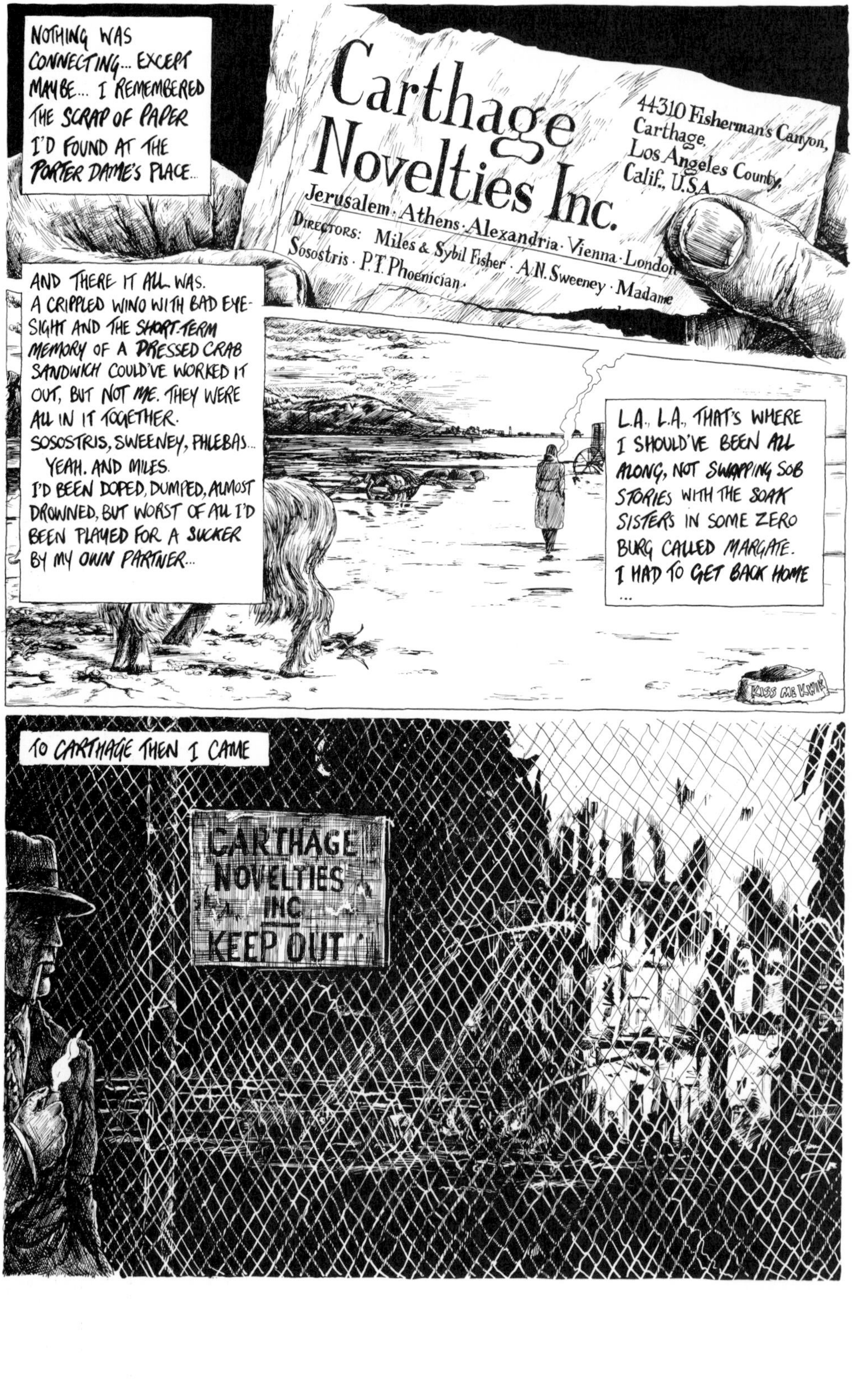
NOTHING WAS CONNECTING... EXCEPT MAYBE... I REMEMBERED THE SCRAP OF PAPER I'D FOUND AT THE PORTER DAME'S PLACE...
Carthage Novelties Inc.
44310 Fisherman's Canyon, Carthage, Los Angeles County, Calif., U.S.A.
Jerusalem · Athens · Alexandria · Vienna · London
Directors: Miles & Sybil Fisher · A.N. Sweeney · Madame Sosostris · P.T. Phoenician ·
AND THERE IT ALL WAS. A CRIPPLED WINO WITH BAD EYE-SIGHT AND THE SHORT-TERM MEMORY OF A DRESSED CRAB SANDWICH COULD'VE WORKED IT OUT, BUT NOT ME. THEY WERE ALL IN IT TOGETHER. SOSOSTRIS, SWEENEY, PHLEBAS... YEAH. AND MILES. I'D BEEN DOPED, DUMPED, ALMOST DROWNED, BUT WORST OF ALL I'D BEEN PLAYED FOR A SUCKER BY MY OWN PARTNER...
L.A., L.A., THAT'S WHERE I SHOULD'VE BEEN ALL ALONG, NOT SWAPPING SOB STORIES WITH THE SOAK SISTERS IN SOME ZERO BURG CALLED MARGATE. I HAD TO GET BACK HOME ...
KISS ME KWIK
TO CARTHAGE THEN I CAME
CARTHAGE NOVELTIES INC
KEEP OUT

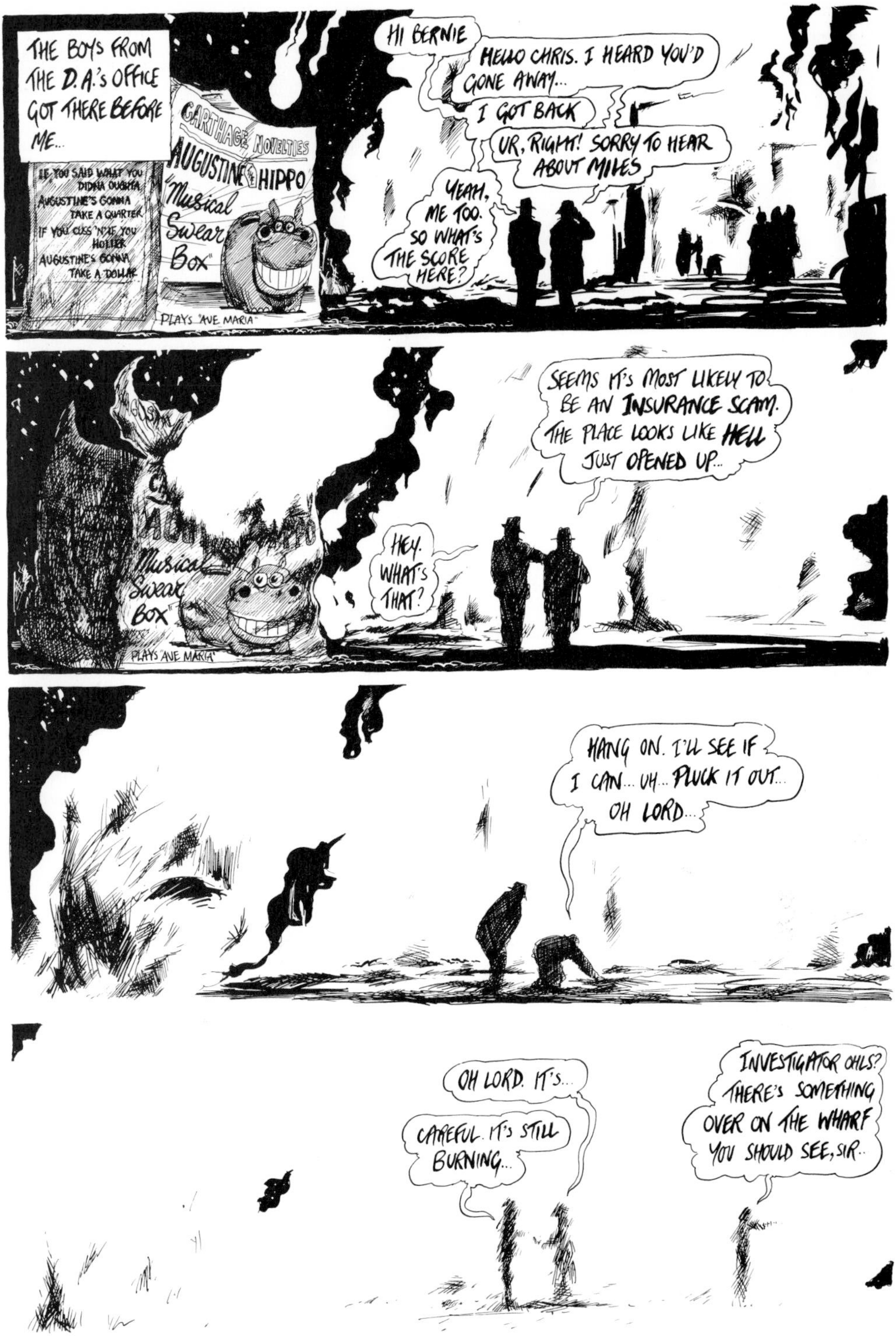
THE BOYS FROM THE D.A.'s OFFICE GOT THERE BEFORE ME...
IF YOU SAID WHAT YOU DIDNA OUGHTA AUGUSTINE'S GONNA TAKE A QUARTER IF YOU CUSS 'N' IF YOU HOLLER AUGUSTINE'S GONNA TAKE A DOLLAR
CARTHAGE NOVELTIES
AUGUSTINE THE HIPPO
"Musical Swear Box"
PLAYS "AVE MARIA"
HI BERNIE
HELLO CHRIS. I HEARD YOU'D GONE AWAY...
I GOT BACK
UR, RIGHT! SORRY TO HEAR ABOUT MILES
YEAH, ME TOO. SO WHAT'S THE SCORE HERE?
SEEMS IT'S MOST LIKELY TO BE AN INSURANCE SCAM. THE PLACE LOOKS LIKE HELL JUST OPENED UP...
Musical Swear Box"
PLAYS "AVE MARIA"
HEY. WHAT'S THAT?
HANG ON. I'LL SEE IF I CAN... UH... PLUCK IT OUT... OH LORD...
OH LORD. IT'S...
CAREFUL. IT'S STILL BURNING...
INVESTIGATOR OHLS? THERE'S SOMETHING OVER ON THE WHARF YOU SHOULD SEE, SIR..

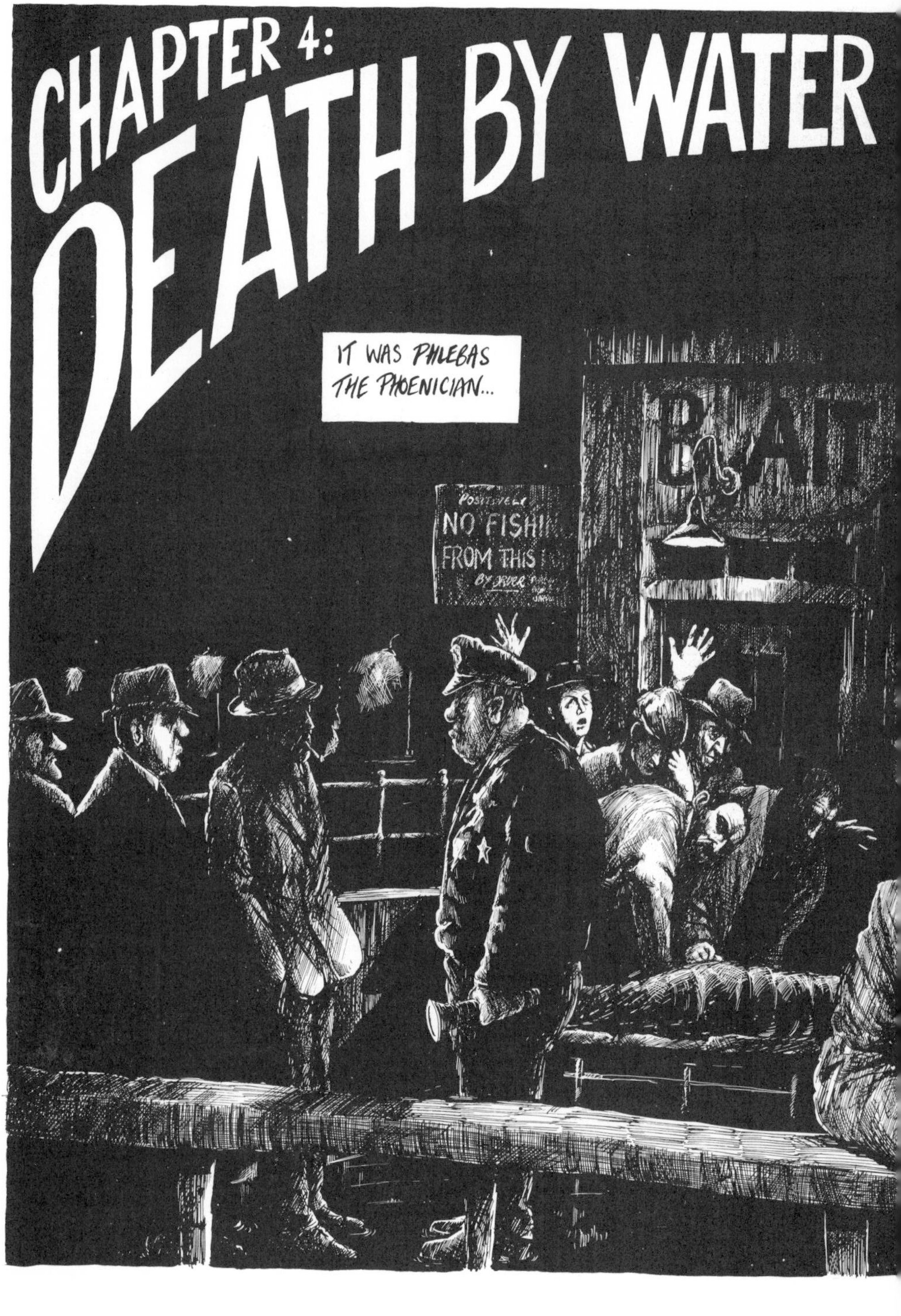
CHAPTER 4:
DEATH BY WATER
IT WAS PHLEBAS THE PHOENICIAN...
NO FISHI
FROM THIS

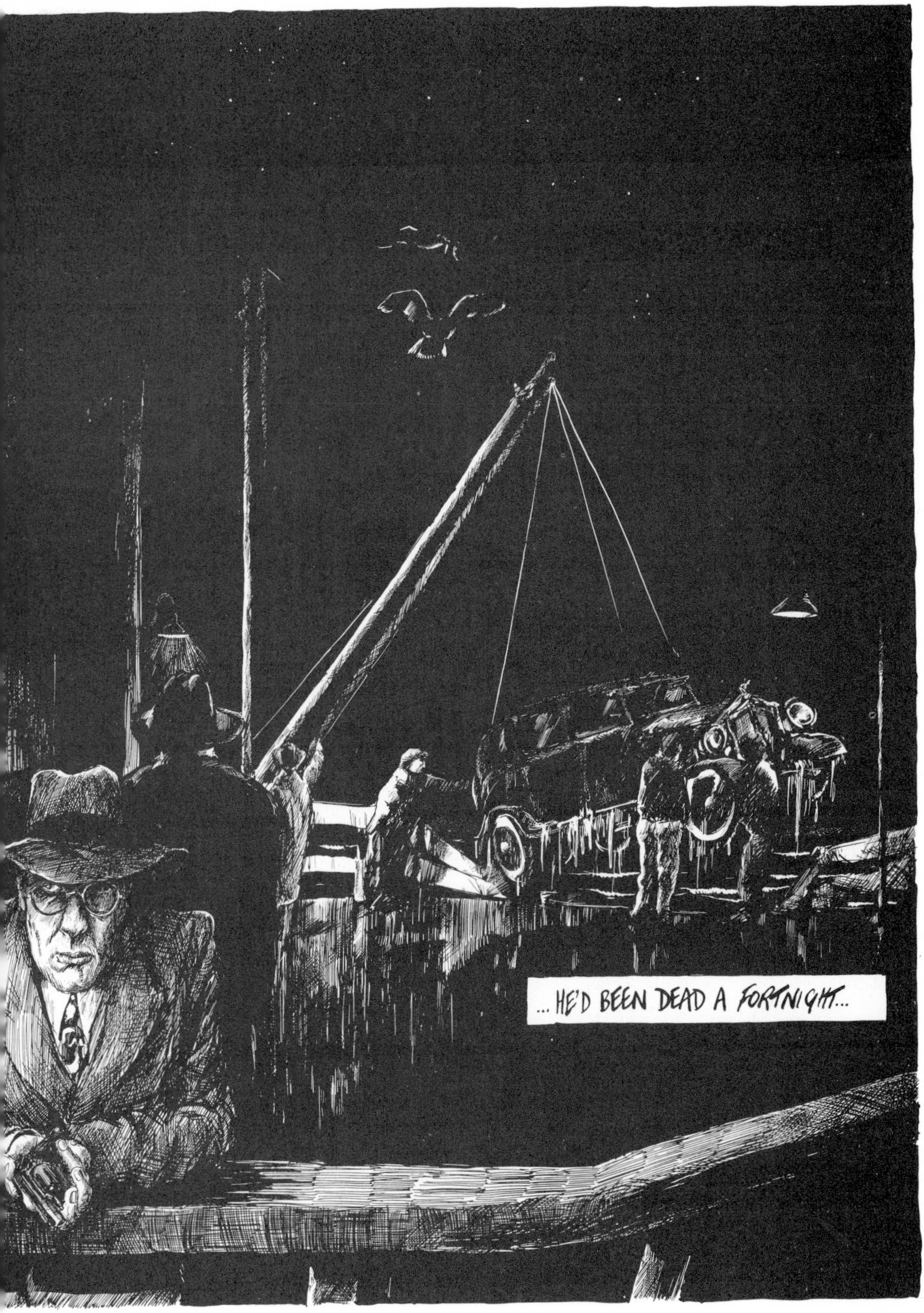
... HE'D BEEN DEAD A FORTNIGHT...

CHAPTER 5: WHAT THE THUNDER SAID

DOESN'T LOOK THE WAY YOU'D HANDLE IT, CHRIS

ME? I DIDN'T DO THIS

WELL...

LOOK AT IT THIS WAY.
WE KNOW FROM HIS I.D. THAT THIS PHLEBAS GUY WORKED, APPARENTLY AS A **CHAUFFEUR**, FOR A DOWN-TOWN **SIDESHOW** ARTIST CALLED **SOSOSTRIS**. NOW IF SHE MAKES A LIVING **SPOOKING SUCKERS**, THAT'S **HER** BUSINESS. WHAT'S **OUR** BUSINESS IS THAT SHE SAYS A **PRIVATE PARTY** SHE WAS THROWING ABOUT A **MONTH** BACK WAS BUSTED UP BY A **GUMSHOE** WHOSE DESCRIPTION **MATCHES YOUR OWN.**
YOU FOLLOWING ME?

THEN WE HEAR FROM **LONDON** THAT THIS SAME SOSOSTRIS' **BUTLER** IS FOUND MURDERED IN A **CATHOUSE**. SOMEBODY SAYS THEY SEE AN AMERICAN **SHAMUS** WHO SOUNDS **KINDA FAMILIAR** LEAVING THE PLACE AT A TIME CORRESPONDING TO THE **KILLING. THEN** THE BRITISH POLICE SAY THEY GET **COMPLAINTS** FROM AN **ALL-GIRL SINGING TROUPE** ABOUT THIS SAME SHAMUS, OR AT LEAST ONE **REMARKABLY SIMILAR**, ASKING QUESTIONS ABOUT, YOU GUESSED IT, THIS **SAME** PHLEBAS.

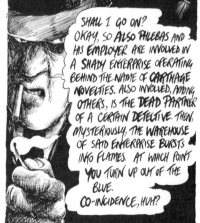

SHALL I GO ON?
OKAY, SO **ALSO** PHLEBAS AND HIS **EMPLOYER** ARE INVOLVED IN A **SHADY ENTERPRISE** OPERATING BEHIND THE NAME OF **CARTHAGE NOVELTIES**. ALSO INVOLVED, AMONG OTHERS, IS THE **DEAD PARTNER** OF A CERTAIN **DETECTIVE.** THEN, MYSTERIOUSLY, THE **WAREHOUSE** OF SAID ENTERPRISE BURSTS INTO FLAMES. AT WHICH POINT **YOU TURN UP** OUT OF THE **BLUE.**
CO-INCIDENCE, HUH?

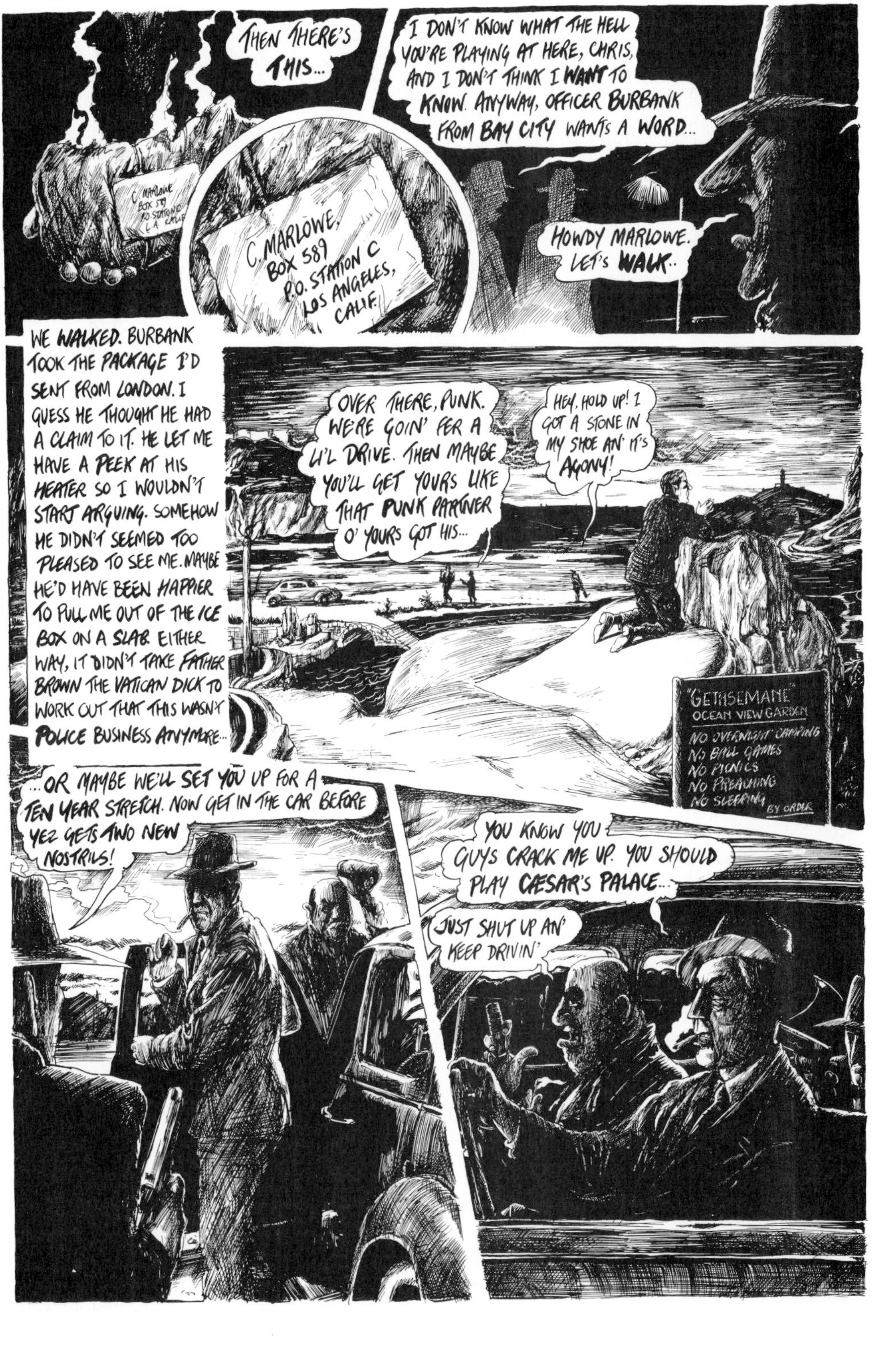
THEN THERE'S THIS...
C. MARLOWE, BOX 589 P.O. STATION C LOS ANGELES, CALIF.
I DON'T KNOW WHAT THE HELL YOU'RE PLAYING AT HERE, CHRIS, AND I DON'T THINK I WANT TO KNOW. ANYWAY, OFFICER BURBANK FROM BAY CITY WANTS A WORD...
HOWDY MARLOWE. LET'S WALK..
WE WALKED. BURBANK TOOK THE PACKAGE I'D SENT FROM LONDON. I GUESS HE THOUGHT HE HAD A CLAIM TO IT. HE LET ME HAVE A PEEK AT HIS HEATER SO I WOULDN'T START ARGUING. SOMEHOW HE DIDN'T SEEMED TOO PLEASED TO SEE ME. MAYBE HE'D HAVE BEEN HAPPIER TO PULL ME OUT OF THE ICE BOX ON A SLAB. EITHER WAY, IT DIDN'T TAKE FATHER BROWN THE VATICAN DICK TO WORK OUT THAT THIS WASN'T POLICE BUSINESS ANYMORE...
OVER THERE, PUNK. WE'RE GOIN' FER A LI'L DRIVE. THEN MAYBE YOU'LL GET YOURS LIKE THAT PUNK PARTNER O' YOURS GOT HIS...
HEY, HOLD UP! I GOT A STONE IN MY SHOE AN' IT'S AGONY!
"GETHSEMANE" OCEAN VIEW GARDEN
NO OVERNIGHT CAMPING
NO BALL GAMES
NO PICNICS
NO PREACHING
NO SLEEPING BY ORDER
...OR MAYBE WE'LL SET YOU UP FOR A TEN YEAR STRETCH. NOW GET IN THE CAR BEFORE YEZ GETS TWO NEW NOSTRILS!
YOU KNOW YOU GUYS CRACK ME UP. YOU SHOULD PLAY CAESAR'S PALACE...
JUST SHUT UP AN' KEEP DRIVIN'

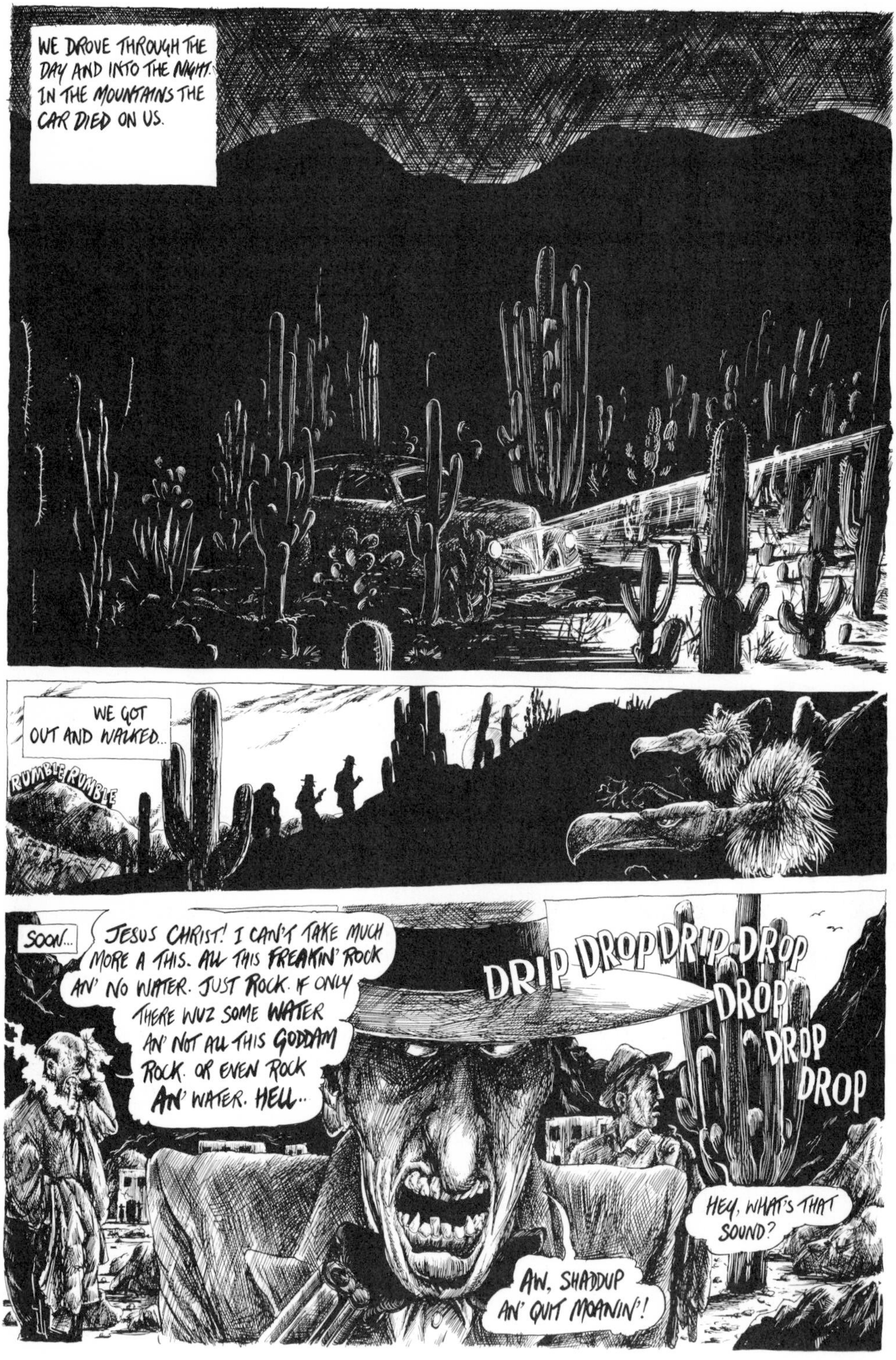
WE DROVE THROUGH THE DAY AND INTO THE NIGHT. IN THE MOUNTAINS THE CAR DIED ON US.
WE GOT OUT AND WALKED...
RUMBLE RUMBLE
SOON...
JESUS CHRIST! I CAN'T TAKE MUCH MORE A THIS. ALL THIS FREAKIN' ROCK AN' NO WATER. JUST ROCK. IF ONLY THERE WUZ SOME WATER AN' NOT ALL THIS GODDAM ROCK. OR EVEN ROCK AN' WATER. HELL...
DRIP DROP DRIP DROP DROP DROP DROP
HEY, WHAT'S THAT SOUND?
AW, SHADDUP AN' QUIT MOANIN'!

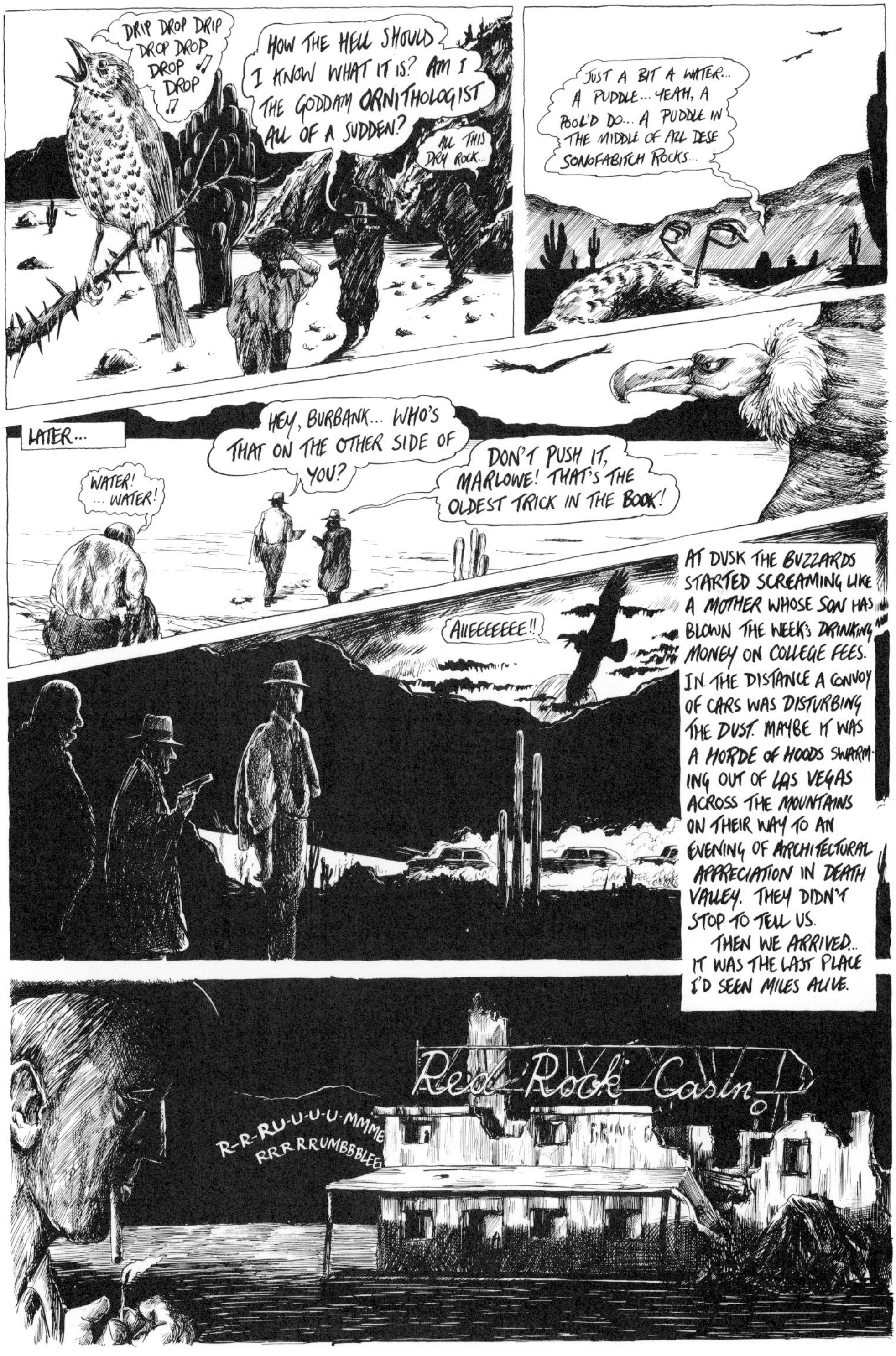
DRIP DROP DRIP DROP DROP DROP DROP
HOW THE HELL SHOULD I KNOW WHAT IT IS? AM I THE GODDAM ORNITHOLOGIST ALL OF A SUDDEN?
ALL THIS DRY ROCK...
JUST A BIT A WATER... A PUDDLE... YEAH, A POOL'D DO... A PUDDLE IN THE MIDDLE OF ALL DESE SONOFABITCH ROCKS...
LATER...
HEY, BURBANK... WHO'S THAT ON THE OTHER SIDE OF YOU?
WATER! ... WATER!
DON'T PUSH IT, MARLOWE! THAT'S THE OLDEST TRICK IN THE BOOK!
AIIEEEEEEE!!
AT DUSK THE BUZZARDS STARTED SCREAMING LIKE A MOTHER WHOSE SON HAS BLOWN THE WEEK'S DRINKING MONEY ON COLLEGE FEES. IN THE DISTANCE A CONVOY OF CARS WAS DISTURBING THE DUST. MAYBE IT WAS A HORDE OF HOODS SWARMING OUT OF LAS VEGAS ACROSS THE MOUNTAINS ON THEIR WAY TO AN EVENING OF ARCHITECTURAL APPRECIATION IN DEATH VALLEY. THEY DIDN'T STOP TO TELL US.
THEN WE ARRIVED... IT WAS THE LAST PLACE I'D SEEN MILES ALIVE.
Red Rock Casino
R-R-RU-U-U-U-MMME RRRRRUMBBBLEE

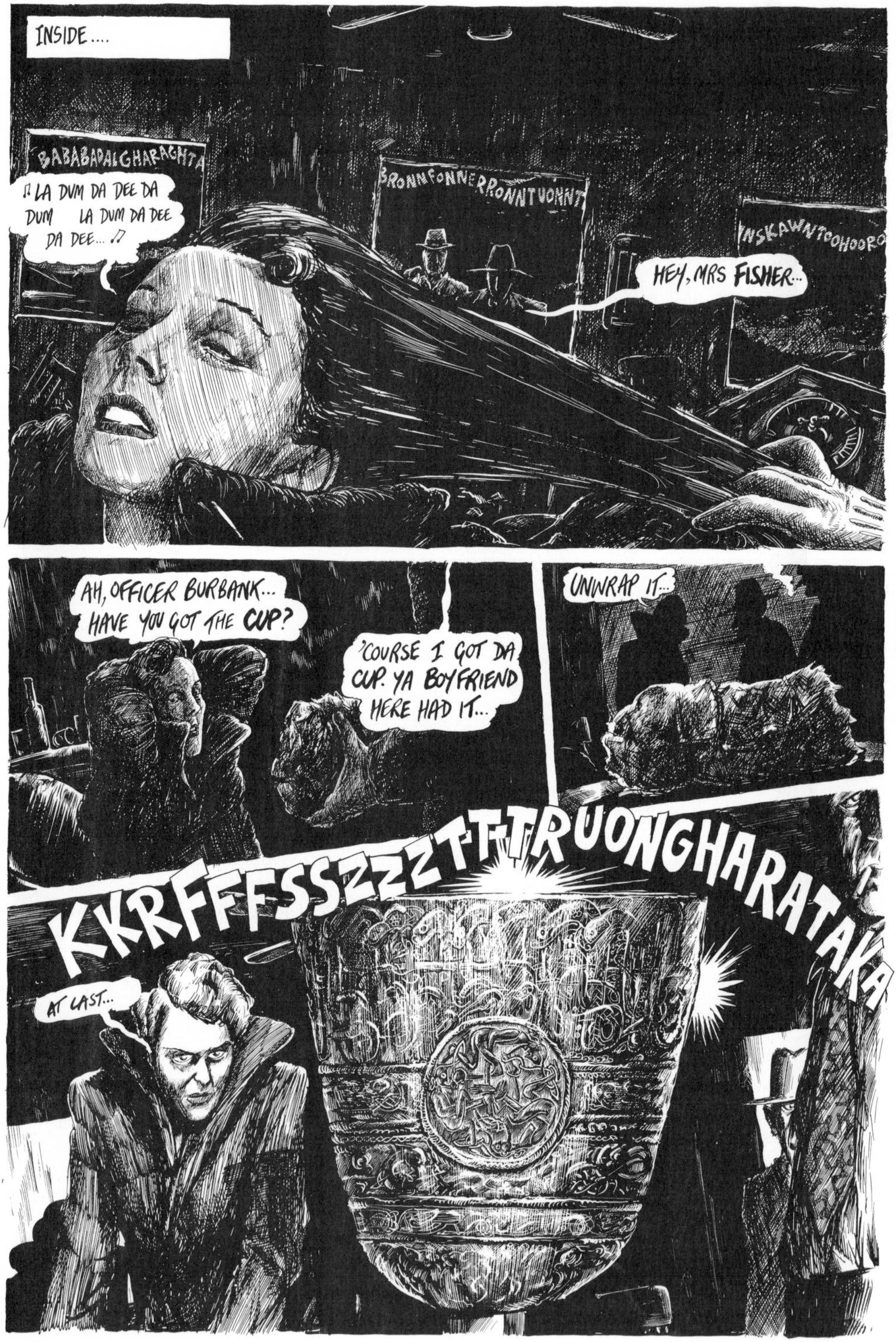
INSIDE....
BABABADALGHARAGHTA
♫ LA DUM DA DEE DA DUM LA DUM DA DEE DA DEE... ♫
BRONNFONNERRONNTUONNT
INSKAWNTOOHOORO
HEY, MRS FISHER...
AH, OFFICER BURBANK... HAVE YOU GOT THE CUP?
'COURSE I GOT DA CUP. YA BOYFRIEND HERE HAD IT...
UNWRAP IT...
KKRFFFSSZZZTTTTRUONGHARATAKA
AT LAST...

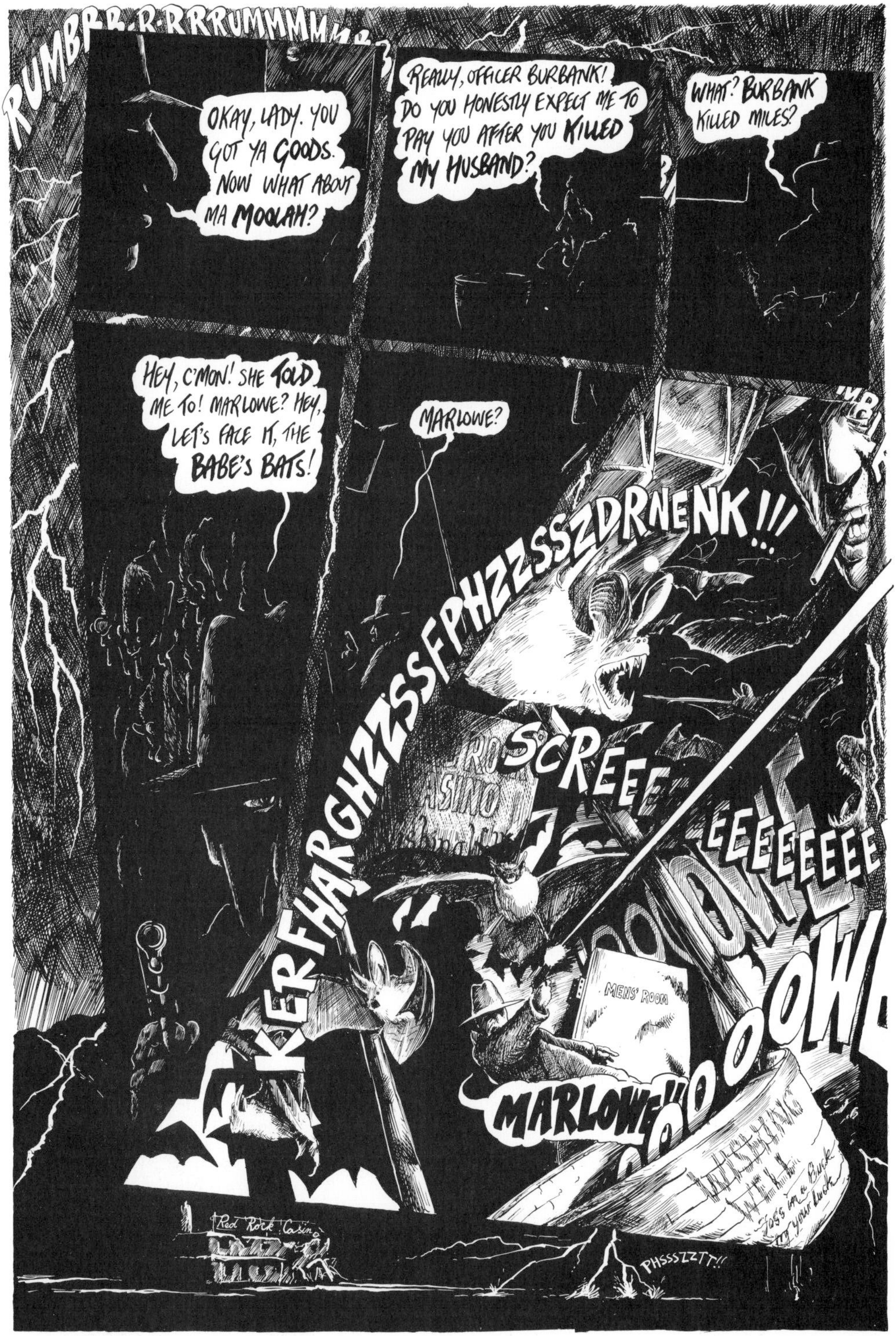
RUMBRR-R-RRRUMMMMMM
OKAY, LADY. YOU GOT YA GOODS. NOW WHAT ABOUT MA MOOLAH?
REALLY, OFFICER BURBANK! DO YOU HONESTLY EXPECT ME TO PAY YOU AFTER YOU KILLED MY HUSBAND?
WHAT? BURBANK KILLED MILES?
HEY, C'MON! SHE TOLD ME TO! MARLOWE? HEY, LET'S FACE IT, THE BABE'S BATS!
MARLOWE?
KERFHARGHZZZSSFPHZZSSZDRNENK!!!
SCREEEEEEEEEEEE
MENS' ROOM
MARLOWE!!
Red Rock Casino
PHSSSZZTT!!

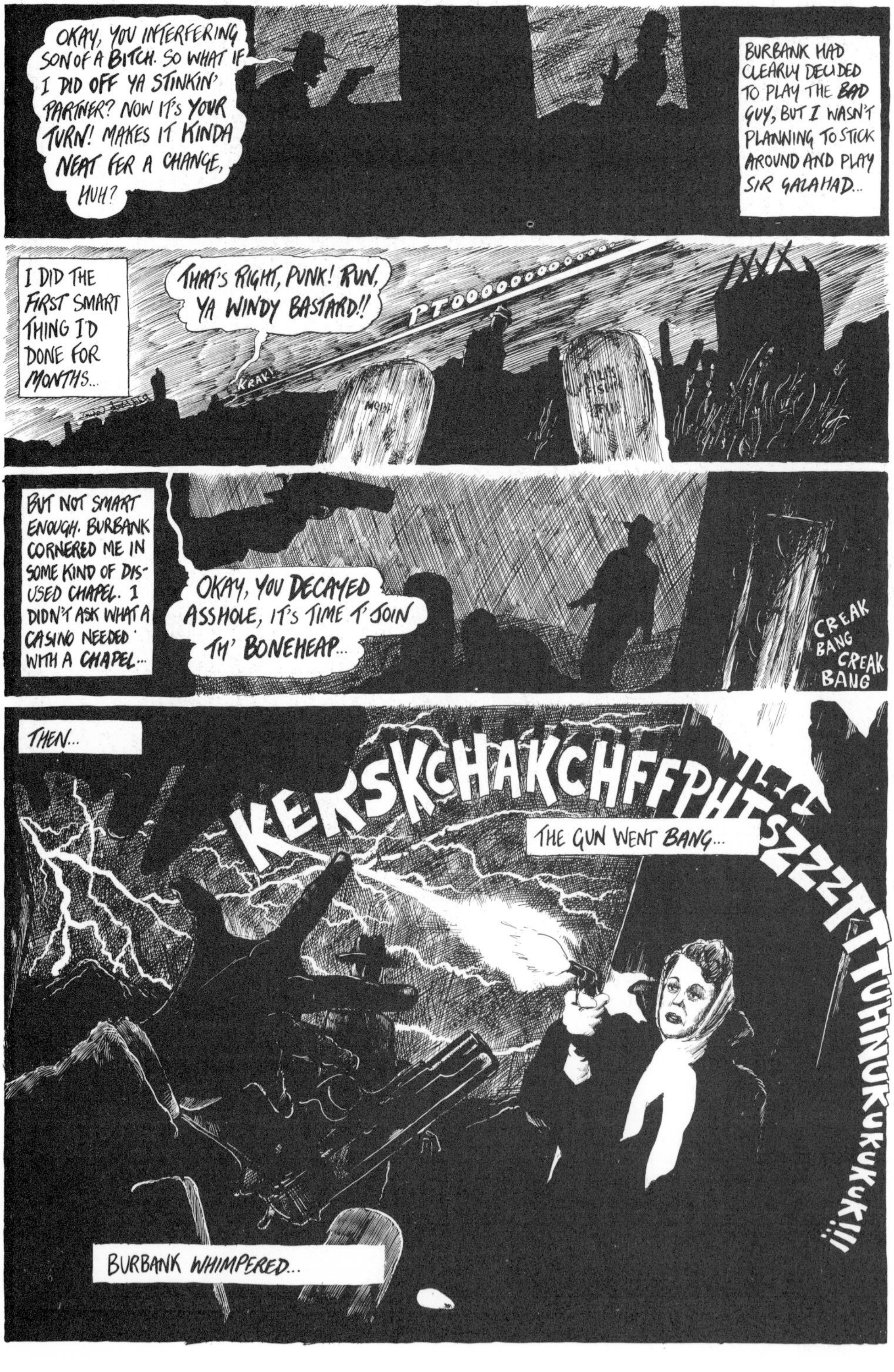
OKAY, YOU INTERFERING SON OF A BITCH. SO WHAT IF I DID OFF YA STINKIN' PARTNER? NOW IT'S YOUR TURN! MAKES IT KINDA NEAT FER A CHANGE, HUH?
BURBANK HAD CLEARLY DECIDED TO PLAY THE BAD GUY, BUT I WASN'T PLANNING TO STICK AROUND AND PLAY SIR GALAHAD...
I DID THE FIRST SMART THING I'D DONE FOR MONTHS...
THAT'S RIGHT, PUNK! RUN, YA WINDY BASTARD!!
KRAK!
PTOOOOOOOOOOOOO
BUT NOT SMART ENOUGH. BURBANK CORNERED ME IN SOME KIND OF DISUSED CHAPEL. I DIDN'T ASK WHAT A CASINO NEEDED WITH A CHAPEL...
OKAY, YOU DECAYED ASSHOLE, IT'S TIME T' JOIN TH' BONEHEAP...
CREAK BANG CREAK BANG
THEN...
KERSKCHAKCHFFPHTSZZZTTTUHNUKUKUKUK!!!
THE GUN WENT BANG...
BURBANK WHIMPERED...

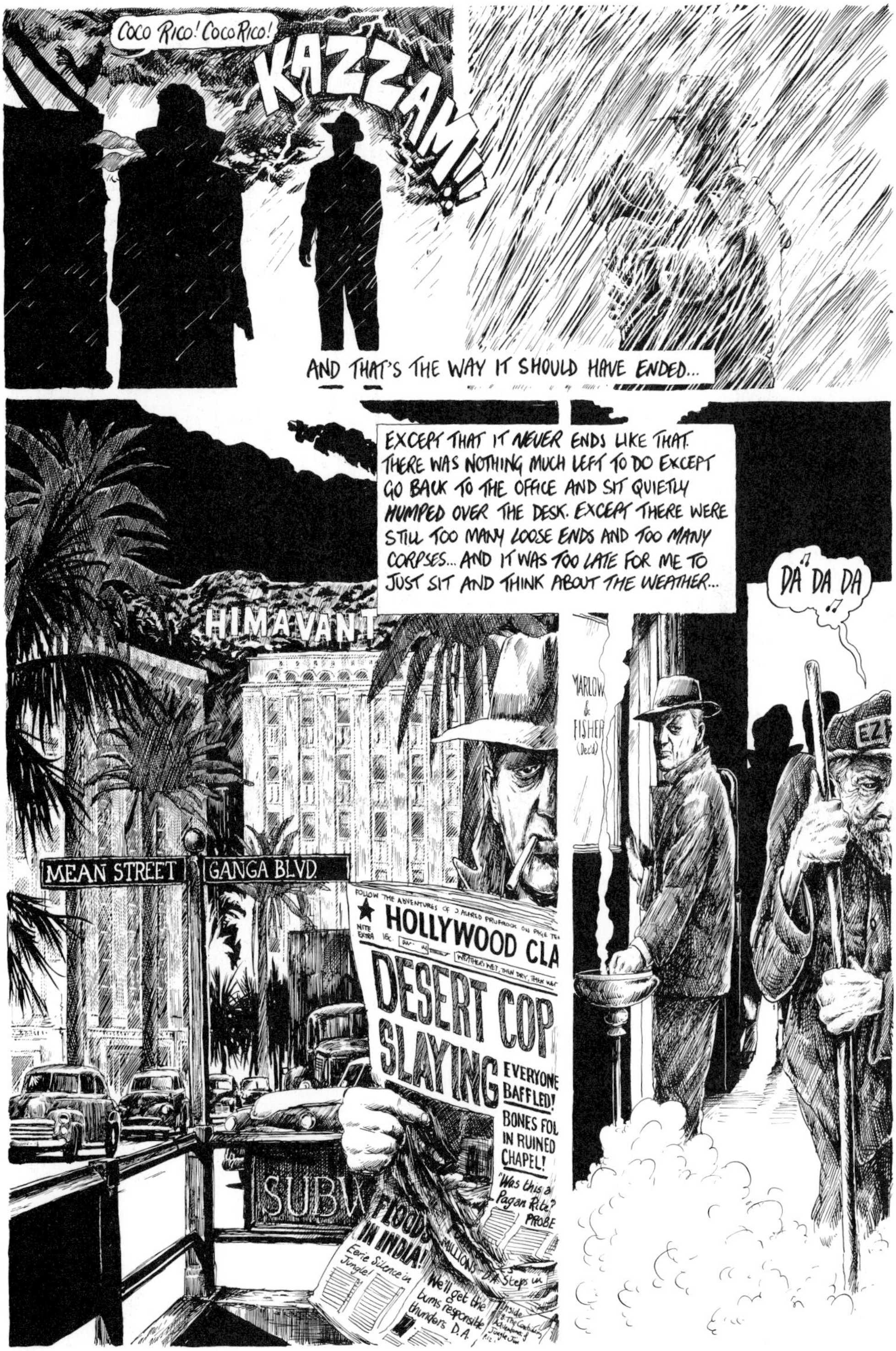
COCO RICO! COCO RICO!
KAZZAM!!
AND THAT'S THE WAY IT SHOULD HAVE ENDED...
EXCEPT THAT IT NEVER ENDS LIKE THAT. THERE WAS NOTHING MUCH LEFT TO DO EXCEPT GO BACK TO THE OFFICE AND SIT QUIETLY HUMPED OVER THE DESK. EXCEPT THERE WERE STILL TOO MANY LOOSE ENDS AND TOO MANY CORPSES... AND IT WAS TOO LATE FOR ME TO JUST SIT AND THINK ABOUT THE WEATHER...
DA DA DA
HIMAVANT
MARLOW & FISHER (Dec'd)
MEAN STREET
GANGA BLVD.
SUBW
FOLLOW THE ADVENTURES OF J. ALFRED PRUFROCK ON PAGE TE
HOLLYWOOD CLA
NITE EXTRA 15¢
WEATHER: WET, THEN DRY, THEN WE
DESERT COP SLAYING
EVERYONE BAFFLED!
BONES FOU IN RUINED CHAPEL!
"Was this a Pagan Rite?" PROBE
FLOODS IN INDIA!
Eerie Silence in Jungle!
MILLIONS
D.A. Steps in
We'll get the bums responsible thunders D.A.

CHRIS...

HI MILES. GLAD TO SEE YOUR LEG'S BETTER

I WAS EXPECTING COMPANY...

CHRIS... WE...

SAVE IT, MILES. THERE'S SOME DATA WE'VE GOT TO DEAL WITH, JUST LIKE GOOD DETECTIVES ARE MEANT TO...

I'VE GIVEN A LOT, BUDDY. A LOT OF HEARTACHE, AND THERE'S STILL A PART OF ME THAT SAYS I SHOULD TURN AWAY FOR A MOMENT AND LET IT GO... BUT IF I DID THAT I MIGHT JUST NOT BE ABLE TO LIVE WITH MYSELF ANYMORE...

MARLOWE

CHRIS...

I STILL DON'T REALLY KNOW WHAT ANY OF THIS HAS BEEN ABOUT, AND EVEN IF I DID I'M NOT TOO SURE I'D CARE ANYMORE. BUT I KNOW IT WAS ENOUGH FOR MY PARTNER TO FAKE HIS DEATH AND LEAVE ME TO PICK UP THE PIECES...

This Week's Deaths

CITY P.I. IN MURDER PROBE

by our Staff reporter

Slain Gumshoe Miles Fisher's partner Chris Marlowe was arrested last night as part of a city-wide manhunt

MURDER DOG SLAY BISHOP

Last night as the Department was enjoying a well earned bone...

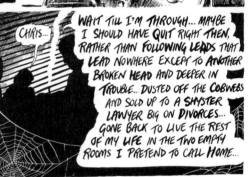

CHRIS...

WAIT TILL I'M THROUGH... MAYBE I SHOULD HAVE QUIT RIGHT THEN, RATHER THAN FOLLOWING LEADS THAT LEAD NOWHERE EXCEPT TO ANOTHER BROKEN HEAD AND DEEPER IN TROUBLE... DUSTED OFF THE COBWEBS AND SOLD UP TO A SHYSTER LAWYER BIG ON DIVORCES... GONE BACK TO LIVE THE REST OF MY LIFE IN THE TWO EMPTY ROOMS I PRETEND TO CALL HOME...

MAYBE I'M JUST CRAZY ENOUGH STILL TO BELIEVE IN OLD FASHIONED THINGS LIKE HONOR AND DOING THE RIGHT THING WHEN EVERYTHING ELSE STINKS...

WHAT'S THAT?

THE D.A., ANGEL. I 'PHONED HIM AS SOON AS I GOT IN. YOU'RE BOTH GOING OVER, AND THAT'S ALL...

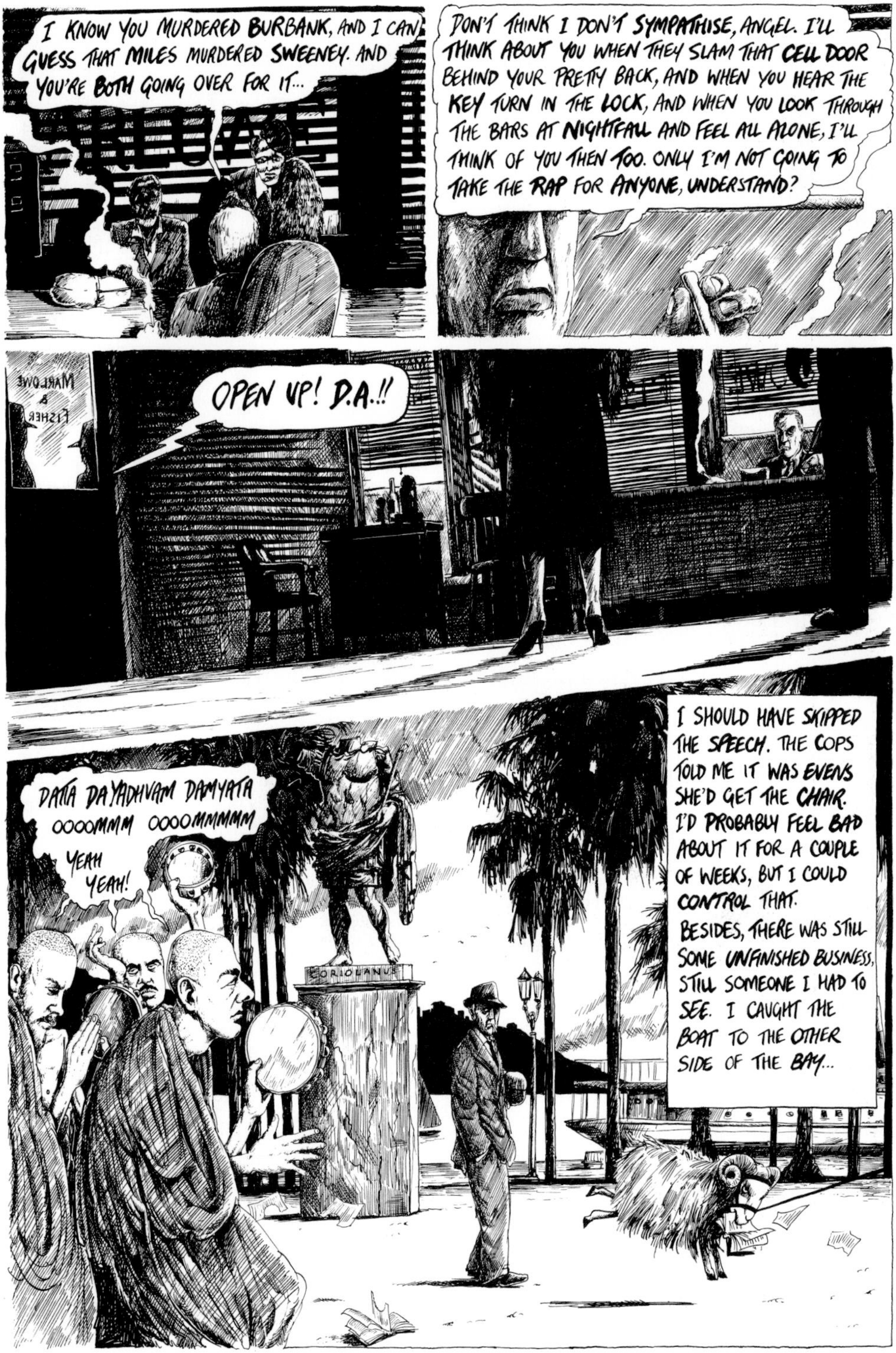
I KNOW YOU MURDERED BURBANK, AND I CAN GUESS THAT MILES MURDERED SWEENEY. AND YOU'RE BOTH GOING OVER FOR IT...
DON'T THINK I DON'T SYMPATHISE, ANGEL. I'LL THINK ABOUT YOU WHEN THEY SLAM THAT CELL DOOR BEHIND YOUR PRETTY BACK, AND WHEN YOU HEAR THE KEY TURN IN THE LOCK, AND WHEN YOU LOOK THROUGH THE BARS AT NIGHTFALL AND FEEL ALL ALONE, I'LL THINK OF YOU THEN TOO. ONLY I'M NOT GOING TO TAKE THE RAP FOR ANYONE, UNDERSTAND?
MARLOWE & FISHER
OPEN UP! D.A.!!
I SHOULD HAVE SKIPPED THE SPEECH. THE COPS TOLD ME IT WAS EVENS SHE'D GET THE CHAIR. I'D PROBABLY FEEL BAD ABOUT IT FOR A COUPLE OF WEEKS, BUT I COULD CONTROL THAT. BESIDES, THERE WAS STILL SOME UNFINISHED BUSINESS, STILL SOMEONE I HAD TO SEE. I CAUGHT THE BOAT TO THE OTHER SIDE OF THE BAY...
DATTA DAYADHVAM DAMYATA OOOOMMM OOOOMMMMM
YEAH YEAH!
CORIOLANUS

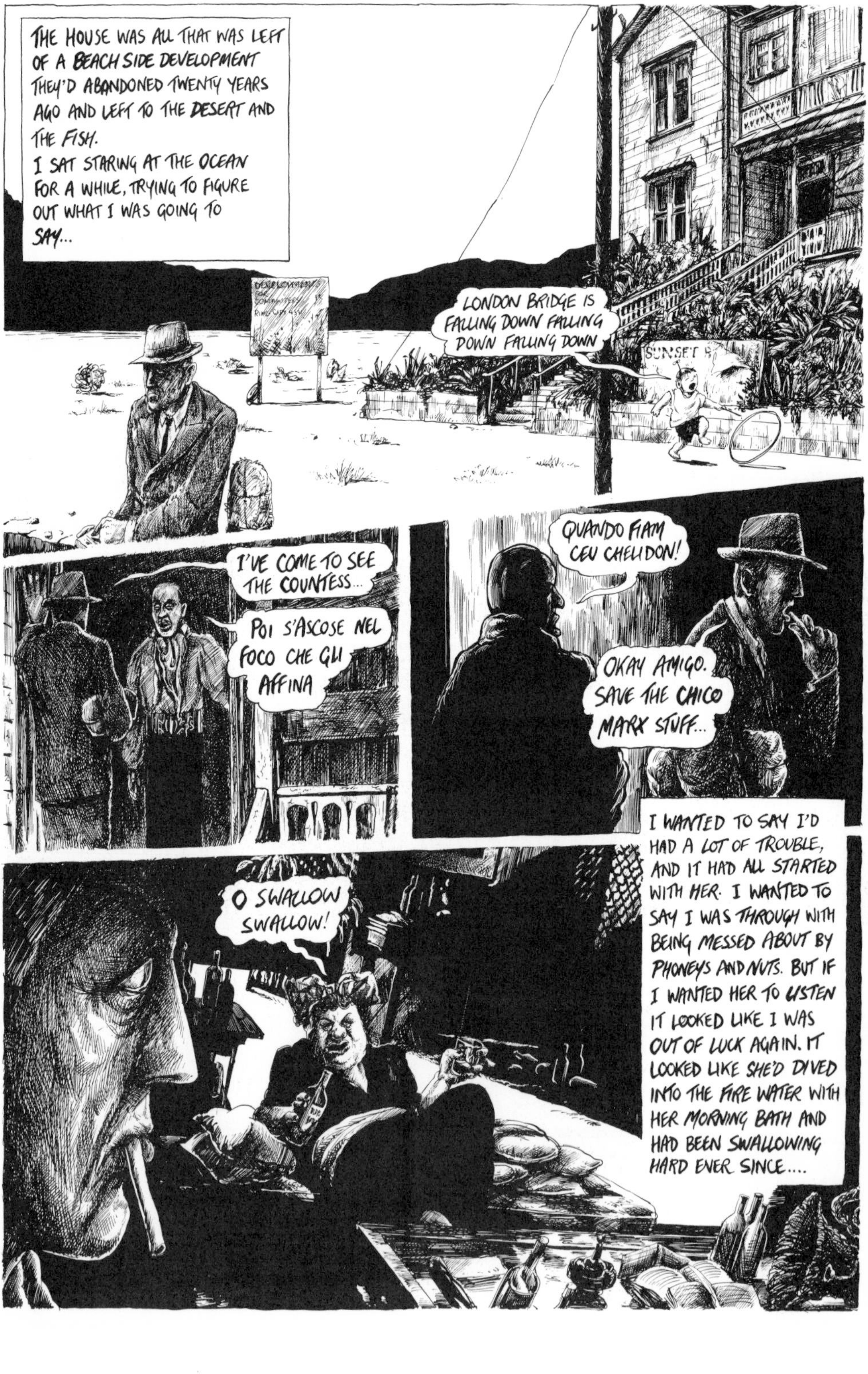
THE HOUSE WAS ALL THAT WAS LEFT OF A BEACH SIDE DEVELOPMENT THEY'D ABANDONED TWENTY YEARS AGO AND LEFT TO THE DESERT AND THE FISH.
I SAT STARING AT THE OCEAN FOR A WHILE, TRYING TO FIGURE OUT WHAT I WAS GOING TO SAY...
LONDON BRIDGE IS FALLING DOWN FALLING DOWN FALLING DOWN
I'VE COME TO SEE THE COUNTESS...
POI S'ASCOSE NEL FOCO CHE GLI AFFINA
QUANDO FIAM CEU CHELIDON!
OKAY AMIGO. SAVE THE CHICO MARX STUFF...
I WANTED TO SAY I'D HAD A LOT OF TROUBLE, AND IT HAD ALL STARTED WITH HER. I WANTED TO SAY I WAS THROUGH WITH BEING MESSED ABOUT BY PHONEYS AND NUTS. BUT IF I WANTED HER TO LISTEN IT LOOKED LIKE I WAS OUT OF LUCK AGAIN. IT LOOKED LIKE SHE'D DIVED INTO THE FIRE WATER WITH HER MORNING BATH AND HAD BEEN SWALLOWING HARD EVER SINCE....
O SWALLOW SWALLOW!

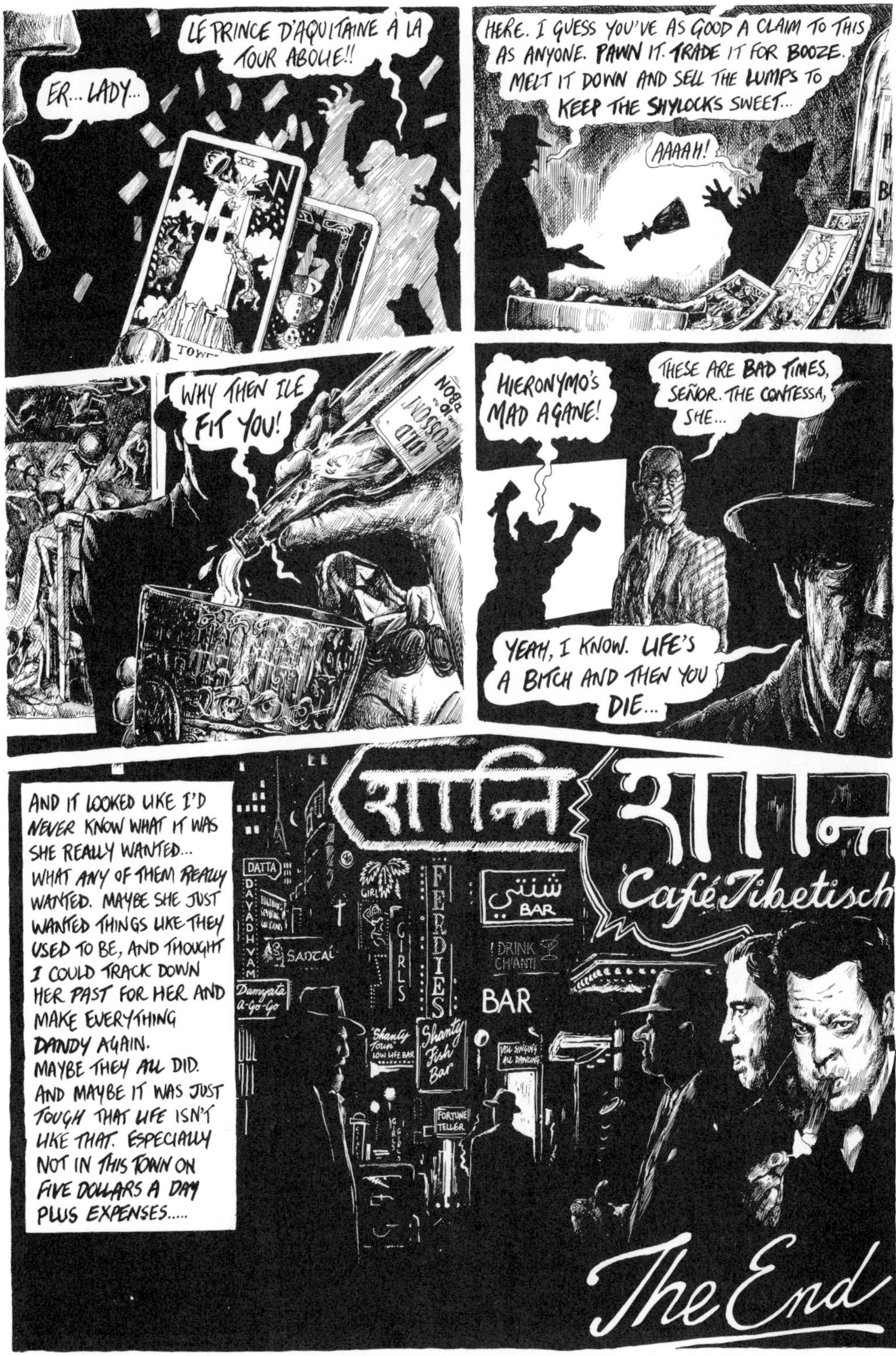
ER... LADY...
LE PRINCE D'AQUITAINE À LA TOUR ABOLIE!!
HERE. I GUESS YOU'VE AS GOOD A CLAIM TO THIS AS ANYONE. PAWN IT. TRADE IT FOR BOOZE. MELT IT DOWN AND SELL THE LUMPS TO KEEP THE SHYLOCKS SWEET...
AAAAH!
WHY THEN ILE FIT YOU!
OLD POSSUM
HIERONYMO'S MAD AGANE!
THESE ARE BAD TIMES, SEÑOR. THE CONTESSA, SHE...
YEAH, I KNOW. LIFE'S A BITCH AND THEN YOU DIE...
AND IT LOOKED LIKE I'D NEVER KNOW WHAT IT WAS SHE REALLY WANTED... WHAT ANY OF THEM REALLY WANTED. MAYBE SHE JUST WANTED THINGS LIKE THEY USED TO BE, AND THOUGHT I COULD TRACK DOWN HER PAST FOR HER AND MAKE EVERYTHING DANDY AGAIN. MAYBE THEY ALL DID. AND MAYBE IT WAS JUST TOUGH THAT LIFE ISN'T LIKE THAT. ESPECIALLY NOT IN THIS TOWN ON FIVE DOLLARS A DAY PLUS EXPENSES.....
DATTA
DAYADHVAM
Damyata A-Go-Go
FERDIES
GIRLS
شنتي
BAR
!DRINK CHIANTI
BAR
Café Tibetisch
Shanty Town Low Life Bar
Shanty Fish Bar
FORTUNE TELLER
The End

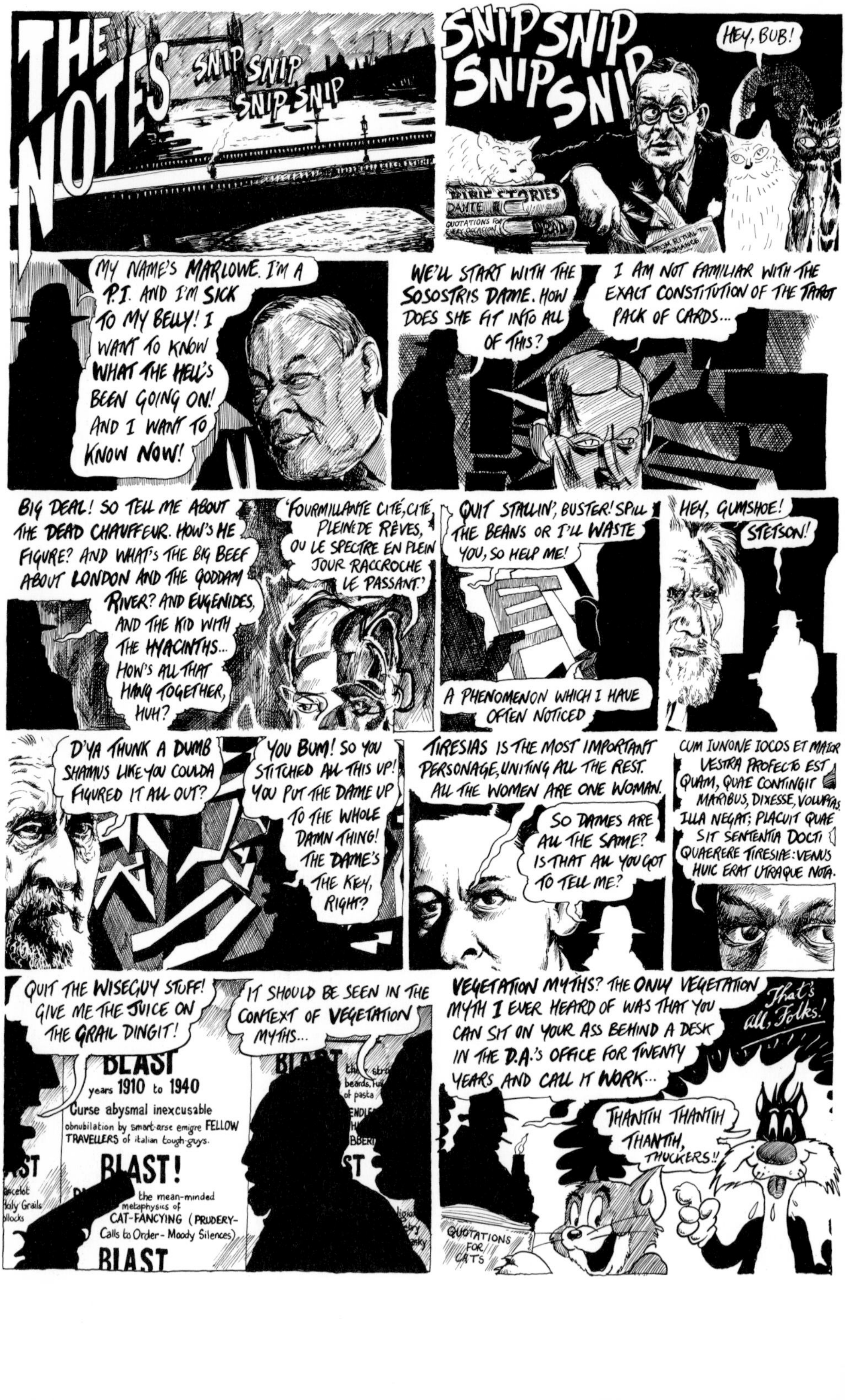
THE NOTES
SNIP SNIP SNIP SNIP
SNIP SNIP SNIP SNIP
HEY, BUB!
DANTE
QUOTATIONS FOR EVERY OCCASION
MY NAME'S MARLOWE. I'M A P.I. AND I'M SICK TO MY BELLY! I WANT TO KNOW WHAT THE HELL'S BEEN GOING ON! AND I WANT TO KNOW NOW!
WE'LL START WITH THE SOSOSTRIS DAME. HOW DOES SHE FIT INTO ALL OF THIS?
I AM NOT FAMILIAR WITH THE EXACT CONSTITUTION OF THE TAROT PACK OF CARDS...
BIG DEAL! SO TELL ME ABOUT THE DEAD CHAUFFEUR. HOW'S HE FIGURE? AND WHAT'S THE BIG BEEF ABOUT LONDON AND THE GODDAM RIVER? AND EUGENIDES, AND THE KID WITH THE HYACINTHS... HOW'S ALL THAT HANG TOGETHER, HUH?
'FOURMILLANTE CITÉ, CITÉ PLEINE DE RÊVES, OU LE SPECTRE EN PLEIN JOUR RACCROCHE LE PASSANT.'
QUIT STALLIN', BUSTER! SPILL THE BEANS OR I'LL WASTE YOU, SO HELP ME!
A PHENOMENON WHICH I HAVE OFTEN NOTICED
HEY, GUMSHOE!
STETSON!
D'YA THUNK A DUMB SHAMUS LIKE YOU COULDA FIGURED IT ALL OUT?
YOU BUM! SO YOU STITCHED ALL THIS UP! YOU PUT THE DAME UP TO THE WHOLE DAMN THING! THE DAME'S THE KEY, RIGHT?
TIRESIAS IS THE MOST IMPORTANT PERSONAGE, UNITING ALL THE REST. ALL THE WOMEN ARE ONE WOMAN.
SO DAMES ARE ALL THE SAME? IS THAT ALL YOU GOT TO TELL ME?
CUM IUNONE IOCOS ET MAIOR VESTRA PROFECTO EST QUAM, QUAE CONTINGIT MARIBUS, DIXESSE, VOLUPTAS. ILLA NEGAT; PLACUIT QUAE SIT SENTENTIA DOCTI QUAERERE TIRESIAE: VENUS HUIC ERAT UTRAQUE NOTA.
QUIT THE WISEGUY STUFF! GIVE ME THE JUICE ON THE GRAIL DINGIT!
IT SHOULD BE SEEN IN THE CONTEXT OF VEGETATION MYTHS...
BLAST
years 1910 to 1940
Curse abysmal inexcusable obnubilation by smart-arse emigre FELLOW TRAVELLERS of italian tough-guys.
BLAST!
the mean-minded metaphysics of CAT-FANCYING (PRUDERY-Calls to Order-Moody Silences)
BLAST
VEGETATION MYTHS? THE ONLY VEGETATION MYTH I EVER HEARD OF WAS THAT YOU CAN SIT ON YOUR ASS BEHIND A DESK IN THE D.A.'S OFFICE FOR TWENTY YEARS AND CALL IT WORK...
That's all, Folks!
THANTIH THANTIH THANTIH, THUCKERS!!
QUOTATIONS FOR CATS

THE
NOTES

Not only the title but the plan and much of the incidental symbolism of this book were suggested by Mr. T. S. Eliot's poem *The Waste Land* (Faber). Indeed, so deeply am I indebted, Mr. Eliot's poem will elucidate the difficulties of the book much better than my notes can do; and I recommend it (apart from the great interest of the poem itself) to any who think such elucidation of the book worth the trouble. To two cinematic works I am indebted in general, both of which have influenced our generation profoundly; I mean *The Big Sleep* and *The Maltese Falcon*. Anyone who is acquainted with these works will immediately recognize in the book certain references to Californian private investigators.

The references are listed by chapter and frame number.

I. THE BURIAL OF THE DEAD

Frame 2. For "dried Tuba," read "dried tuber" throughout.

    17. V. Julian Sykes Wolsey's 1935 poem "On a Bus with J. Alfred Prufrock":

> "In the room the women came and went
> "Talking of Vermeer of Ghent.
> "In the room the women take a hike
> "Talking of Jan van Eyck.
> "In the room the women catch a bus
> "Talking of Walter Gropius.
> "In the room the women leave by train
> "Talking of Michelangelo again."

Also of interest is the minimalist poet D. N. Eva's

> "I knew a man called T. S. Eliot
> "Who wanted to write the 'Waist Land' but couldn't spelliot."

    32. Saint Mary Woolnoth is a City Church designed by Nicholas Hawksmoor, the subject of a novel by Peter Ackroyd, author of *T. S. Eliot* (1984).

II. A GAME OF CHESS

Frames 25 & 26. For further details on the musical notation used here, cf. page 130 of "American Folk Songs" (Penguin, 1964). See also A. L. Morton's *The English Utopia* (East Berlin: Seven Seas Books) and Helen Killane's *The Songs of Burl Ives: Jarring Notes Towards a Definition of the American Male* (Mucho Macho Press).

    36. One is reminded here of W. H. Auden's memorable near-palindrome: "T. Eliot, top bard, notes putrid tang emanating: I'd assign it a name, gnat dirt upset on a drab pot toilet."

    37. Curiously enough, Millais' "Sir Isumbras at the Ford" was Tenniel's model for the White Knight in *Through the Looking Glass*.

III. THE FIRE SERMON

Frames 11–26. I forget which of Eliot's poems these characters originally appear in, but I think one of the early ones.

Cf. *Special Issue Small Arms of World War Two*, ed. Roy Castle (War Action Library, 1981).

26. Peggy Guggenheim's dog, "Sir Herbert Reid," is buried in her garden in Venice.

Cf. Isaac Guillespie's "Eliot with an Angelus, Pound with a Fasces" from *Waiting at the Archduke's* (1934):

> Dada wouldn't buy me a Bauhaus
> Dada wouldn't buy me a Bauhaus
> Vortecism and De Stijl
> Only make me feel quite ill
> And I'd rather have a Bau bau Haus. (my translation)

33. "The Chalice from the Palace." Cf. *The Court Jester* starring Danny Kaye. The Holy Grail should not be confused with Mrs. Llewellyn Lockridge Grayle in *Farewell My Lovely.*

59. Peter Ackroyd is the author of a biography of T. S. Eliot.

65. "He said he was a friend of Wrinkled Doug's." Although a mere pun and not indeed a "joke," this is yet the most important gag in the book, uniting all the rest. Reflecting on the whole section, we might do well to temper Petronius's

> Foeda est in coitu et brevis voluptas
> Et taedat Veneris statim peractae

with Voltaire's highly significant comment

> Il est plaisant qu'on fait une vertu du vice de chasteté; et voilà encore une drôle de chasteté que celle qui mène tout droit les hommes au péché d'Onan, est les filles aux pâles couleurs!

and of equally great anthropological interest is this passage from Empson's inaugural lecture as Professor of English at Sheffield:

> I was rather pleased one year in China when I had a course on modern poetry, *The Waste Land* and all that, and at the end a student wrote in a most friendly way to explain why he wasn't taking the exam. It wasn't that he couldn't understand *The Waste Land*, he said, in fact after my lectures the poem was perfectly clear: but it had turned out to be disgusting nonsense, and he had decided to join the engineering department. Now there a teacher is bound to feel solid satisfaction; he is getting definite results.

80. "Abie the Fishman." The true identity, in the Marx Brothers' film *Animal Crackers*, of the emigré Czech financier Roscoe W. Chandler. The narrative of the film involves the theft of a priceless work of art.

98. Carthage, California. Not to be confused with Carthage, Montana, or Carthage, Texas.

IV. DEATH BY WATER

During the filming of *The Big Sleep*, Bogart asked the director of the picture the significance of the dead chauffeur in the Packard dredged out of the ocean. Not knowing the answer, the director asked the scriptwriters. Equally in the dark, they phoned Chandler, who'd forgotten.

V. WHAT THE THUNDER SAID

In the first part of Chapter 5 three themes are employed: the journey from *The Treasure of the Sierra Madre*, the sound effects at the beginning of *Finnegan's Wake*, and images from the Tex Avery classic *What's Buzzin', Buzzard*.

Frames 1–10. The absence here of a previously dominant figure in the Eliot version is significant, and indicative of how far we've come. Cf. Nietzsche, *Die Fröhliche Wissenschaft*:

> Gott ist tot; aber so wie die Art der Menschen ist, wird as vielleicht noch jahrtausendlang Höhlen geben, in denen man seinen Schatten zeigt....Der christliche Entschluss, die Welt Hässlich und schlecht zu finden, hat die Welt hässlich und schlecht gemacht.

Cf. McLuhan, *Understanding Media*. Also, Bakunin:

если Бог существует, то мы бы должны были Его уничтожить

14. In fact, rather than being a *Turdus aonalaschkae pallasii*, the bird shown here is a *Turdus philomelos*. One presumes that Eliot could equally well have employed the symbolism of, say, a rock hopper penguin at this point. Cf. Kevin Killane, *The Bestiary: Zoos, Zoo Animals and the Weltschmertz* (Pathfinder, 1982).

20. "I am half sick of shadows, said the Lady of Shallot" by John Waterhouse.

29. V. Tennyson, *Maud*.

48. The goat here is probably a misreading of "boat." V. Thomas of Celano:

> Inter oves locum praesta
> Et ab haedis me sequestra
> Statuens in parte dextra.

52. "Le Prince d'Aquitaine à la tour abolie." V. *El Desdichado* by Gerard de Nerval. De Nerval kept a pet lobster which he would take for walks on a leash in the Bois de Boulogne. When asked why, he replied: "It does not bark, and knows the secrets of the sea."

CAST

Chris Marlowe .... Himself

Miles Fisher, his partner........................ Himself

Burbank & Bleistein, Bay City Vice Squad Officers .. Themselves

Countess Marie Larisch .... Herself

The Hyacinth Kid .... Herself

Bernie Ohls, D.A.'s Department Investigator .... Himself

Madame Sosostris, a clairvoyante................. Herself

Sweeney, her butler .... Himself

Sybil Fisher .... Mary Astor

Gunsel/Young Man Carbuncular .... Elisha Cook Jr.

Mr. Eugenides, the Smyrna Merchant .... Sydney Greenstreet

The Thames Daughters......................... Dorothy Comingore
Lauren Bacall
Marlene Dietrich

Tiresias/Woman in Art Gallery .... Dame Edith Sitwell

Janitor/Stetson/Man in Museum/Stetson .... Ezra Pound

Taxi Driver .... Peter Ackroyd

1st Barman..................................... Craig Raine

2nd Barman.................................... Ernest Hemingway

Barflies in 1st Pub....... Richard Aldington, William Carlos Williams,
Henri Gaudier Brezska, John Quinn, W. B.
Yeats, Joseph Conrad, Wyndham Lewis,
Vivienne Eliot, Louis Zukofsky, and T. S. Eliot

Piano Player.................................... Ford Madox Ford

Mandolin Player .... W. B. Yeats

Barflies in 2nd Pub...... Gertrude Stein, Edmund Wilson, Alice B.
Toklas, Robert Graves, Robert Frost, Herman
Melville, and Norman Mailer

Daytrippers on Boat..... Richard Wagner, Aldous Huxley, Henry
James, Lord Robert Dudley, Earl of Leicester,
Dante Alighieri, Elizabeth I, William
Shakespeare, Edmund Spenser, Joseph
Conrad, and William Carlos Williams

Countess Larisch's Houseboy .... Mendy Menendez

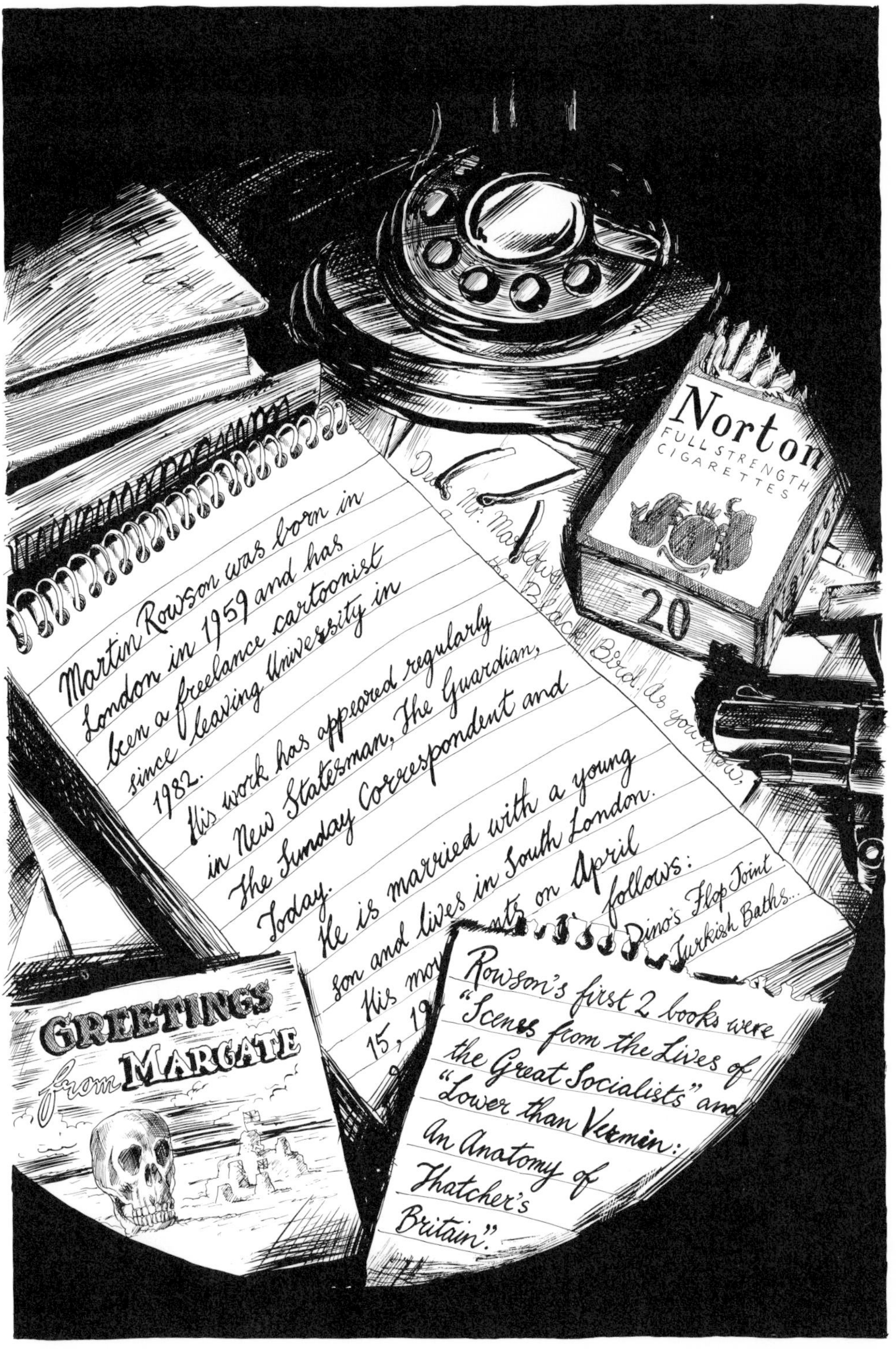
Martin Rowson was born in London in 1959 and has been a freelance cartoonist since leaving University in 1982.
His work has appeared regularly in New Statesman, The Guardian, The Sunday Correspondent and Today.
He is married with a young son and lives in South London.
His mov
15, 19
follows:
Norton
FULL STRENGTH
CIGARETTES
20
Dear Mr. Marlowe
the Black Bird. As you know,
Dino's Flop Joint
Turkish Baths...
Rowson's first 2 books were "Scenes from the Lives of the Great Socialists" and "Lower than Vermin: An Anatomy of Thatcher's Britain".
GREETINGS from MARGATE